"The Most Dismal Times"
William Rowbottom's Diary
Part I   1787-1799

Transcribed and Annotated by Alan Peat

Introduction by Michael Winstanley

Illustrations compiled by Terry Berry

selling at 1.25 pounds for a penny or 12/- to 18/- a load, more than twice the price old potatoes had fetched just three months earlier. Although prices fell back a little in the autumn, another poor harvest ensured that they remained high until well into 1796.

Relatively good harvests in 1796, 1797 and 1798 saw prices return to more normal levels; in the spring of 1797, for example, flour was selling for just 1/8d a peck, potatoes at 3/9d a load. But 1799 was to prove the worse year of the century. 'One of the longest winters ever known by the oldest person living' meant that little could be sown and what was planted failed to grow. By May, there was already 'a great scarcity of food' and everything was 'extremely dear and scarce! Meal and flour is rising very fast.' Cold, wet weather continued into July, hitting the potato crop and making 'every necessary of life . . . extremely dear'. August was much the same, seriously affecting the quality and quantity of hay which could be cut. Autumn saw no let up in the dreadful conditions. By October Rowbottom's despair plumbed new depths:

> 'The season still continues so wet and cold that the fruits of the Earth are all blighted, crippled or starved for a great deal of flowers and grain have never ripened or come to perfection but have withered away, the same as untimely buds which sometimes bud at Christmas. Roses, Honeysuckle and a deal of flowering shrubs have perished before they fully blowed or ripened. The air is cold as in December. The Earth is wet and soft as in a wet January. Everything has the most terrific and gloomy appearance such as never was known before . . . what must become of the poor? God have mercy on us.'

By November children were crying in the streets for bread. Corn, much of it irretrievably damaged, was still standing in the fields in December. 1800, unfortunately for the poor, was to prove no better. These, he concluded, were indeed, 'the most dismal times'.

Rowbottom's view that price rises were the inevitable consequence of natural causes was not universally shared, probably because, as one farmer observed in John Holt's *General View of the Agriculture of the County of Lancaster*, published in 1795, regarding 'the cultivation of land, and its produce, with ten or twelve miles of Manchester, the people know nothing'. Widespread 'riots' broke out, not just in Oldham, Saddleworth and Delph, but all over England in the summer of 1795, the autumn of 1799 and again the following year. These have attracted widespread attention from historians who have concluded that they were far from 'riots' in the sense of being the unplanned, indiscriminate, desperate actions of a violent mob intent on seizing food at any cost. They enjoyed the support of a wide cross-section of society, although they were often dominated, as at Delph, by 'tumultuous women'. Notice was often given of their intention to take action if their demands for fair prices were not met. Those involved clearly felt that market speculators were profiting unjustly from the plight of the poor and they consequently attacked those dealers who were regarded as having breached unwritten codes of conduct which defined customary responsibilities and duties towards the members of the communities in which they lived. The rioters did not object *per se* to the operation of a free market but they did demand that it was tempered by what has come to be known as a 'moral economy'. Flour and meal, therefore, were not stolen; they were sold to members of the crowd at what was considered to be a fair price, similar to that prevailing under normal conditions, and the proceeds returned to the dealer involved. Outside major towns like Manchester, where such crowd action was possibly more violent and seen as a major threat to civil order by the authorities, local magistrates, like Sir Watts Horton (although not it would seem Joseph Pickford of Royton Hall), clearly sympathised with the plight of the poor. They pleaded with dealers (or badgers) to lower their prices, although to no avail if Rowbottom's record is anything to go by since they resorted to the deployment of cavalry in the end.

Historians have adduced from such activity, and from the growing resentment of oppressive manufacturers evident even in Rowbottom's diary, that previously widely shared, communal notions of right and wrong were being abandoned by the commercial classes who were profiting or, some might say, profiteering from the expansion of the market. Whether growing antipathy towards such men by the expanding class of industrial wage earners was gradually transformed into an increasingly articulate, class consciousness towards the end of the decade, which was to dictate the pattern of social relations and political relations well into the following century, remains a fiercely contested point. There is no doubt, however, that the underlying growth and changes in the structure of the region's major industries combined with the severity of trade depressions and food crises, served to heighten social tension within the local community.

Revolution, War and Repression

These tensions were further exacerbated by events overseas. The French Revolution of July 1789 set in train a series of events which was to lead to over a generation of virtually continuous war and domestic repression. The newly formed republic's success seemingly challenged the political and social principles which underpinned Britain's constitution and social order at home by giving hope to those who championed radical political change, while threatening the country's national security and commerce overseas. Fear of sedition and revolution had rocked British society even before the execution of Louis XVI, his family and countless 'enemies of the state' in January 1793 and the outbreak of war between Britain and France the following month. The formation of various societies throughout the country during 1791 and 1792 campaigning for constitutional reform, and the publication of Tom Paine's *The Rights of Man*, the second volume of which sold over 200,000 copies in 1792, caused widespread panic among the authorities. In May 1792 George III issued a proclamation against 'Seditious Writings', while locally JPs refused to renew the licences of publicans who were known to have allowed allegedly subversive meetings on their premises. 'Church and King' mobs in a number of cities, especially Birmingham in July 1792 and Manchester in December 1792, attacked the property of persons associated with the reform movement. Once war had broken out, expressions of loyalty became even more pronounced and thousands of men enrolled to fight for their country in the first few months of hostilities. Government repression at home increased as decisive military success proved elusive and casualties mounted, leading to disillusionment with the war while adding credence to reformers' criticisms of those who waged it. Habeas Corpus was suspended in April 1794, spies were hired to collect information to sustain prosecutions brought against prominent reformers, the Seditious Meetings Act and Treasonable Practices Act were passed in 1795, trade unions were outlawed in the Combination Acts of 1799 and 1800, and both the regular army and the local militia were deployed to maintain order.

Rowbottom was an astute observer of how this profoundly affected the lives of ordinary people in Oldham during the period. Prior to the middle of 1792 his concerns had been largely parochial; not even the French Revolution of 1789 occasioned remark. The increasing frequency with which he refers to political events thereafter, however, suggests a growing consciousness of the outside world and its importance, brought about not just by the press, but through the dispersal of many of Oldham's male population throughout Europe and the Americas.

In Oldham, as in neighbouring Manchester, loyalist reaction rather than support for reform would appear to have been the initial response to these events. The annual anti-Catholic, patriotic celebrations of 5 November took on added significance. Paine's effigy was solemnly hung and burnt on New Year's Day 1793 and news of the outbreak of war prompted disparaging remarks about the composition of the French armies ('. . . have a great deal of women in them who act both as officers and privates'). The following month saw the beginning of the flood of army recruits which persisted well into 1794, attracted by 'the pant in the path of Glory' and the allurements of uniform, stirring music and financial bounty. There was a clamour for oak boughs to decorate house doors on 29 May, a customary expression of patriotism, with boughs selling for as much as 1/6d (15p) in Manchester. Military victories were the cause of public celebrations in the town. Such events seemingly touched every family, even William's brother George enlisting on 12 April 1794 and being sent to serve in Ireland.

The increasing disillusionment on the part of many of the population with the government in Westminster is also evident, however. Although there is nothing in his diary to suggest that he had republican or reforming principles, and much indeed to suggest strong attachment to the established social order personified locally by Sir Watts Horton of Chadderton Hall, even Rowbottom is clearly not without sympathy for the small group of parliamentary reformers critical of the government, led by John Knight. These tried to hold a public meeting in Royton on Easter Monday 1794 but were 'inhumanely treated by a merciless mob'. The 'Jacobins' were also 'insulted by ignorant, impudent blaggards' at Oldham fair in May the following year. He was also aware that poverty was potentially a more powerful inducement to recruitment than unalloyed patriotism and that the departure of so many married men often left their wives and families destitute and dependent on parish relief. As reports of casualties mounted into 1795, enthusiasm for war evaporated; the end of May saw 'the branches of the verdant oak more free from rapine . . . in Manchester this year there was no demand'. When armed cavalry were called in to escort arrested food rioters in July, they were stoned by the local populace. By 1797 opponents of the war were clearly more confident, publicly refusing to deck their doors with oak and, although military victories late in the year were again the occasion of celebration, there was clearly widespread dissatisfaction with the government and only the return of economic depression revived recruitment in 1799.

Conclusion

The end of the century did not herald a turning point in either the country's or Oldham's fortunes; the trends established in the 1790s continued to be evident. Despite a brief, welcome respite during the uneasy peace secured in 1802, during which there was a boom reminiscent of the profitable heyday of the early 1790s, military hostilities dragged on for another decade and a half, disrupting trade and threatening food supplies. Textile manufacture continued to increase its dominance over the local economy, the establishment of more steam and water powered spinning mills helping to promote employment, although not to improve the handloom weavers' situation which continued to deteriorate even before the power loom's widespread adoption in the 1820s. By this decade, Oldham was beginning to establish its superiority over its neighbouring townships and the settlement on the hill was taking on the appearance of an industrial town, while the new manufacturing classes were beginning to challenge the older landed order which had prevailed in Rowbottom's youth. Fortunately for the historian, Rowbottom survived for another thirty years and continued to record his impressions of these dramatic transformations, but that, as they say, is another story.

Select Bibliography and Further Reading

Oldham

E. Butterworth, *History of Oldham* (1849, rpt with additions, 1856, E. J. Morten, Manchester, 1981) remains the best general introduction to the area in this period although both K. McPhillips, *Oldham: the formative years* (Neil Richardson, Swinton, nd) and Hartley Bateson, *A Centenary History of Oldham* (Oldham Borough Council, 1949) contain valuable material. Both J. Aikin, *A Description of the Country Thirty to Forty Miles round Manchester* (1795, rp David & Charles, Newton Abbot, 1968) and E. Baines, *History, Directory and Gazetteer of the County Palatine of Lancaster* (2 vols, Liverpool, 1824, rp, David & Charles, Newton Abbot, 1968) and the same author's mammoth *A History of Lancashire* (4 volumes 1836) are informative contemporary descriptions. R. Poole, 'Oldham Wakes' in J. K. Walton and J. Walvin (eds), *Leisure in Britain, 1780-1939* (Manchester University Press, 1983) is an excellent account of the major festive occasion of the year while S. Bamford, *Early Days* (1849, rp Frank Cass, 1967) is a vivid description of life in neighbouring Middleton; there is a recent biography of the author which sets his life and work into context, M. Garratt, *Samuel Bamford: portrait of a radical* (George Kelsall, Littleborough, 1992). J. Foster, *Class Struggle and the Industrial Revolution* (Methuen, 1974) contains some information on the 1790s, but is a difficult, controversial and flawed book.

Cotton Textiles and the Handloom Weavers

A. P. Wadsworth and J. de L. Mann, *The Cotton Trade and Industrial Lancashire, 1600-1780* (Manchester University Press, 1931), although dated and ending just before the period covered by Rowbottom is still the best introduction to the growth and complexity of cotton in the county. M. M. Edwards, *The Growth of the British Cotton Trade, 1780-1815* (Manchester University Press, 1967) and D. A. Farnie, *The English Cotton Industry and the World Market, 1815-1896* (Oxford University Press, 1979) are excellent studies which contain much on domestic and international aspects of the industry. G. W. Daniels, 'The cotton trade during the Revolutionary and Napoleonic War', *Transactions of the Manchester Statistical Society*, 1915-16, pp. 53-84 deals specifically with this period.

Handloom weavers have been the subject of two extended studies by D. Bythell, *The Handloom Weavers* (Cambridge University Press, 1969) and G. Timmins, *The Last Shift: the decline of handloom weaving in nineteenth-century Lancashire* (Manchester University Press, 1993), although neither deals in detail with the late 18th century. E. P. Thompson's passionate, influential book, *The Making of the English Working Class* (Victor Gollancz, 1963; Penguin Books, 1968) has much on the weavers and their plight, as well as a mass of material on the late 18th century in general. R. Glen, *Urban Workers in the early Industrial Revolution* (Croom Helm, Beckenham, 1983) is primarily about Stockport, but contains comparative material on, and discussion of, handloom weavers.

Farming and Food Riots

J. Holt, *General View of the Agriculture of the County of Lancaster* (1795) is the standard source for the state of farming and diet prior to the major problems of the decade. R. A. E. Wells, *Wretched Faces: Famine in Wartime England, 1793-1803* (Alan Sutton, Gloucester, 1988) is a detailed monograph on the national problem and the responses to it. General studies of food riots include E. P. Thompson, 'The moral economy of the English crowd in the eighteenth century', *Past and Present*, vol 50, 1971, pp. 76-136 and J. Stevenson, 'Foot riots in England, 1792-1818', in J. Stevenson and R. Quinalt (eds), *Popular Protest and Public Order* (Longman, London, 1974). A. Booth, 'Food riots in the North-West of England, 1790-1801', *Past and Present*, vol 77, 1977, pp. 84-107 deals generally with their causes and manifestations in Lancashire while J. Bohstedt, *Riots and Community Politics in England and Wales, 1790-1810* (Harvard University Press, 1983) argues strongly that riots in Manchester did not fit the pattern elsewhere.

War and Revolution

Among the many detailed studies of the period, C. Emsley, *British Society and the French Wars, 1793-1815* (Macmillan, Basingstoke, 1979) stands out as a readable account which takes into account the social impact, while H. T. Dickinson (ed), *Britain and the French Revolution, 1789-1815* (Macmillan, Basingstoke, 1989) contains brief articles on political, diplomatic and military aspects of the war. The same author's *British Radicalism and the French Revolution, 1793-1815* (Oxford University Press, 1985) offers a succinct résumé of recent debates.

General Background

For a broader context E. J. Evans, *The Forging of the Modern State: early industrial Britain, 1783-1870* (Longman, London, 1983, 2nd ed. 1995) is an accessible textbook. J. K. Walton, *Lancashire: a social history, 1558-1939* (Manchester University Press, 1987) is an unrivalled county history.

POPULATION FIGURES: OLDHAM TOWNSHIPS, 1789-1811

	Oldham	Chadderton	Royton	Crompton	Total
1789*	8012	2404	1584	1916	13916
1792*	9480	2512	1728	2056	15776
1801	12024	3452	2719	3482	21677
1811	16690	4133	3910	4746	29479

AVERAGE ANNUAL POPULATION GROWTH RATES

	Oldham	Chadderton	Royton	Crompton	Total
1789–1792	6.11%	1.50%	3.03%	2.44%	4.46%
1792–1801	2.98%	4.16%	6.37%	7.71%	4.16%
1801–1811	3.88%	1.97%	4.38%	3.63%	3.60%

TOTAL POPULATION GROWTH, 1789-1811

	Oldham	Chadderton	Royton	Crompton	Total
1789–1811	108.31%	71.92%	146.84%	147.70%	111.84%

* Estimated figures for 1789 and 1792 derived by multiplying the number of households in each township by a factor of four.

William Rowbottom's Diary 1787–1797
1787 & 1788

From latter end of June 1787 to the latter end of August 1787 was one of the wettest Hay Harvests ever known by the oldest person living, it raining the greatest part of those days.

November 2nd 1787 for 3 weeks of last past excessive wet weather.

October 27th 1787. William Scofield of Grotton Head in Saddleworth unfortunately fell into a coal pit in Greenacres. He languished six hours and then died. He was fifteen years old and if youth would be more cautious when in any place of danger it would stop the mouths of those who are apt to say he had no business at all there. He fell in as he was imprudently standing at the eye of the pit.

On the night of November 5th 1787 was one of the most tremendous nights for rain

Chadderton Hall

accompanied with vivid flashes of lightning that was ever seen. Nothing could stop the velocity of the water for it swept down all bridges etc. before it. At Chadderton Hall it burst all the Fish ponds in the Shrubbery. Salford bridge was taken and a man was drowned as he was standing looking over one side of it.

Onions were sold this year 3 lb per penny. Courser sort 4 lb per penny in November 1787.

December 12th 1787 died wife of James Ogden, schoolmaster of Oldham. Ann wife of John Lowe of Oldham age(d) 26 years (and) Esther, wife of Jonathan Neild of Oldham.

Old Halkyard of Greenacres died December 18th 1787 age 97. Anne Fitton, Keeper of the 'Hare and Hounds' Inn in Berry (Bury) hanged herself on Sunday 16th December 1787. She was relict of Joseph Fitton who was unfortunately killed along with three other persons in a barn where a company of players were acting in June last.

Smethurst James, of Oldham, Cotton Twister died December 27th 1787.

Marlor of Oldham, a Chelsea pensioner, he lost his hand on the Expedition to Carthagena (*1) under Admiral Vernon; died January 1st 1788. He was commonly called "Stump Marlor".

Raynor, wife of Thomas, of "Old Clarks" died in an advanced age, January 12th 1788.

Lees William, of Oldham an old veteran belonging to Chelsea Hospital died December 12th 1788.

Taylor of Middleton was stricken over the loins with a carrot that weighed 1 pound 6 ounces of which wound he died, was buried Middleton January 28th 1788

> 'A thousand ways there is on Earth
> For to deprive poor man of breath.'

Whittaker, wife of Mr. Samuel Whittaker, (Chandler of Oldham) died of a violent cancer in her breast, February 1788.

Bamford Mary relict of the late Andrew Bamford, Innkeeper Church Lane Oldham. Died February 2nd 1788.

Taylor John, of Cockhouse Fold, Oldham, died February 17th 1788 age 57.

Adam Stock of Stake Hill was buried February 20th 1788. The distress of his family is great they being ill of the Fever and his wife ignorant of his death.

Travis John, of Royton, Gentleman. Died February 24th 1788.

Bardsley Titus, Stonemason of Bottom of Maggot-lane. Died February 28th 1788 age 77.

Mellor Mary, relict of the late Samuel of Hargreaves; she died at Lees Hall February 29th 1788 age 72.

Wild Josuah, formerley of Foomurt and commonly called Foomaurt Joss died at Oldham Workhouse March 3rd 1788.

Lees Hannah, daughter of the late Robert Lees of Maggot-Lane died March 4th 1788 age 18 of a consumption.

Bell Betty of the Township of Chadderton, single woman, being taken in labour at Alkrington Wood, instead of coming to Chadderton Workhouse to lay in wait went to Jumbo near Middleton, the residence of James Wisherwood the father of her child. There she was delivered and there she did and would lay in on the 26th February 1788. She afterwards married James Wisherwood.

Chadwick Anna, wife of Austin Chadwick died at Robert Lees' Maggot- lane of a consumption, March 11th 1788, age 24.

Fire at Isaac Hardy's at Newroe which burnt 6 pounds of cotton, 5 pairs of stockings, set the cradle on fire with a child in which was much burnt. It happened through the wife imprudently holding the candle under the cotton as it was drying (*2). March 6th 1788.

Buckly Elizabeth, daughter of Doctor Buckly of Chadderton Heights died after a long illness, March 22nd 1788.

Oldham Workhouse

Page 8

Snow, a large fall to the depth of 9 inches all over the country and a frost for the space of 12 days. March 6th 1788.

A man killed in a coal pit by the rope breaking as he was going down at Doghill, Crompton, March 20th 1788.

Barlow, wife of Ben Barlow, clockmaker and formerly keeper of the Nag's Head Inn in Oldham died at Cowhill March 25th 1788.

Broadbent James, of Glodwick returning home much intoxicated unfortunately fell into a coal-pit and was killed, his wife buried on the 26th February last. They have left 4 children March 26th 1788.

Page 9

Roger Anne of Scolesfold died October 16th 1787.

Rowbottom John, broke his arm as he was returning home from Hopwood Hall by falling off the bridge at Spring Brook near his house at Hunt-lane. April 3rd 1788.

Cow died of George Wood's of Northmoor valued at 12s 9d, April 8th 1788.

Dalsey Isaac Ogden Governor of Chadderton Workhouse was struck with the palsey so that he fell to the ground as he was standing at the butchers in Oldham April 5th 1788.

Duelling. Mr. John Clegg of Manchester, Cotton Manufacturer, came to Oldham and challenged on Monday February 18th 1788 . . .

Page 10

. . . Mr. William Brennand, Doctor of Physic, to fight him with sword and pistol. Mr. Clegg was prepared with those dreadful weapons. The doctor was not behind in neither courage nor resolution not anything fit to equip a gentleman dueller save arms, which he received from a neighbouring gentleman. But however by the interference of their friends the affair was amicably settled to the satisfaction of both parties without the effusion of any crimson gore.

Lees James, of Stotfield died in an advanced age April l9th 1788.

Stang-riding (*3). Peter Blaze of North Moor rode Stang for . . .

Page 11

. . . Amos Ogden of same place, April 22nd 1788. What is remarkable (is that) Amos rode Stang for Peter in the year 1776.

Murder and Robbery

Mr. George Worthington of Werneth was most inhumanely shot dead. There were a quantity of slugs extracted from the wound which was in his left breast. A sum of money and a silver watch, a pair of spectacles taken from his person. He was shot at 2 mile stone betwixt Manchester and Oldham. March 29th 1788.

Page 12

Elopements in the month of April 1788. Mary wife of George Fyldes of Lane Ends near Denton eloped. She was the daughter of James Travis of Cowhill.

William Heywood eloped from his wife Jane; from Newroe.

Mary, wife of James Taylor eloped from their house at a Ulnnock and did take with her his silver watch and two suits of clothes belonging to her said husband. This affair happened April 18th 1788.

April 19th 1788, James Heanthorn, commonly called 'Blamey' was for . . .

Oldham stocks

Page 13

. . . his bad behaviour committed to the Stocks in Oldham at 9 of the clock at night and broke out at 4 o clock morning. Was taken again the next day, said he knew who shot Worthington and that he was one of the murderers but it was proved where he was at the time the murder was committed and that his story was nothing but artful villany mixed with knavery.

John Hall, Collier of Oldham was much bruised and leg and thigh broke in a coal pit near Horsedge-Fold, May 3rd 1788.

Clegg Sarah, wife of Joseph Clegg . . .

Page 14

. . . of Mumps, Cotton manufacturer died at a very early age, May 6th 1788.

Lees John, formerly Keeper of the Nags Head Inn in Oldham died May 19th 1788.

Butterworth Ann of Craigh near Chadderton died in an advanced age May 22nd 1788.

May 22nd, this day one Mayal of Greenacres-Moor owing to a fever not being in his senses took the opportunity while his wife went on an errand to drown himself in the Mill dam at Waterhead Mill. Likewise Old Jim Knot had nearly put an end to his existence by the help of a cord but was prevented time enough to save his life. This affair happened in Bent.

Bent

Page 15

Thursday May 15th 1788. A person narrowly escaped being killed on Kersal Moor.

Peggy, wife of Mr. James Hobson, Mercer and Draper of Oldham died May 28th 1788.

Greaves Alice, a woman hanged herself at Mickelhurst, Ashton parish on the 28th May 1788, aged betwixt 50 and 60.

Buckley, Ann, wife of James Buckly of Beartrees died of a Consumption, June 2nd 1788.

Nield Sally, of Oldham died young of a Consumption, June 2nd 1788.

George Newton of Bent had his foot nearly crushed off by a great quantity of Earth falling on him as he was getting sand near Lees Hall, June 2nd 1788.

Page 16

June 1st 1788, a person very much disturbed Congregation at Oldham Church this day, but on strict examination it proved he was affected with the Hydrophobia.

June 1788. Onions sold at 3 pence per pound and Hops 3 shilling per pound.

Chadwick, Jonathan, Milnwright, died a Burnley Yatte June 9th 1788 age 82 years.

Newton John, Stonemason of Oldham died June 13th 1788 age disorder, a violent fever.

June 17th 1788. An uncommon hot day and on the 18th an uncommon loud crack of thunder. The thunderbolt fell at Hargreaves near Oldham but happily did no damage.

North east view of Oldham Church from Horse Hedge about 1780

Page 17

Taylor James, died at Hollinwood, June 18th 1788. Age 87.

A lamentable misfortune on the 27th June 1788. John Morris and Joseph Booth were in winding out of a coal pit, Broadway Lane. A stone fell out of the side of the pit and killed Booth dead in the tub. Morris was taken home alive but died that night. Morris lived in Nathan Roe Oldham, and left a wife and large family to bemoan their loss. He, while living, was an honest, industrious sober man. Booth was a Yorkshireman and married the widow of the one Roscoe who was . . .

Page 18

. . . killed in a coalpit on the 23rd November 1785. They were both universally lamented.

From the beginning of April to the later end of June 1788 was a severe drought attended with uncommon heat.

James Barlow, clockmaker of Oldham was interred at Oldham, June 22nd 1788.

A child of Simeon Holdings of Holden Fold much bruised on its head by the kick of a horse July 5th 1788.

Thorp Thomas, commonly called Tom of Jammeys, of Hollinwood was buried at Oldham, July 21st 1788.

A child of James Horsfalls of Oldham was unfortunately killed by a cartwheel going over its head, July 22nd 1788.

Page 19

Oldham John Mr., of Stakil died suddenly in an advanced age, July 21 1788.

A child of William Beswicks, joiner of Oldham died raving mad through having the misfortune of being bitten by a mad dog. Age 4 years old. July 31st 1788.

Whittaker Ralph, died suddenly at Scolesfold Maggot-lane, August 3rd 1788.

Burkit Thomas, of Horsedge Fold was buried at Oldham, August 6th 1788.

July 31st 1788, a man run from Blakely to Knotsford and once round the Racecourse . . .

Page 20

. . . and back again in 7 hours 1 half and a few minutes for half a guinea. He run naked and afforded a deal of diversion.

The Bishop of Chester passed through Burnley-lane on his way to Liddyate where he consecrated the chapel at Liddyate, August 15th 1788.

Whitehead Nicholas of Brook near Bullsteak died at an early age of a disorder that was then very prevalent all over the country. August 19th 1788.

Stock, wife of the late Adam Stock of Stakell (see page 5) died after languishing since February. Died August 23rd 1788.

Page 21

Rodes William of Brow, near Cowhill, after being tortured for upwards of 5 years with the French pox died in the greatest agonies, August 21st 1788.

Lees John, leg broke and much bruised in a marlpit of Mr. Abraham Cleggs of Lane End, August 28th 1788.

Heap Thomas, Collier of Oldham, much bruised in a coalpit at Edge Lane.

Jackson James, formerly an Oxford Blue, died after a long and tedious illness at Chadderton Workhouse, September 2nd 1788.

Ogden Alice, wife of James Ogden, shoemaker of Busk died after a long illness in an advanced age. September 6th 1788 Age 66.

Page 22

Duckworth Joseph, formerly of Burnley Lane died at Chadderton Workhouse aged 82. September 13th 1788.

Michael Rowbottom and James Rowland had the misfortune to be much bruised in returning from Manchester, the latter by falling off his horse and the former in assisting him to mount was thrown from his horse and very dangerously bruised. August 26th 1788.

Much robbing of orchards in this month of September 1788, for on the night of the 19th some daring villains robbed Mrs.Taylor's orchard and in order to be secure they fastened the doors of Mrs. Taylor's and Neddy Cheetham. And the following evening some villains broke into the henroost belonging to the late Edmund Wolstencroft of Coldhurst Lane stole the bodies of 3 hens and one cock and left the heads in the roost.

Page 23

Wolsoncroft Martha, relect of the late Edmund Woolsoncroft of Coldhurst Lane died September 24th 1788.

In the month of August 1788 the disorder called the influenza prevailed very much all over England and there died some few. They were affected by a great pain in their limbs, a sore throat, and in recovering they were subject to sweat prodigiously, and the flesh wasted astonishingly and left them very weak and low.

Robbery. Edmund Simpson of Humphrey Lane, returning from Manchester, was attacked by two footpads, who with pistol and severe threats robbed him of his watch and three guineas in money, September 27th 1788.

Page 24

Samuel Barlow of Henhouse, Royton, robbed on the new road near Werneth of some money. October 1st 1788.

Howard John, of Hilltop Chadderton, a considerable swailer died October 4th 1788. Disorder and fever.

Jackson James, commonly called "Old Greens" died July 1st 1788.

From February 1788 to October 1788 the Fustian Branch received a severe stab owing to so many houses failing and those that stood their ground taking advantage and grieviously oppressing the poor.

William Horton Esquire of Chadderton, his birthday and age 21 years October 21st 1788.

Page 25

Wednesday October 22nd 1788, this being the yearly day at Oldham Mr. Fawcett preached before the members of the Sick Club Societies from Thessilonians 2nd, 3rd Chapter and 10th verse, and uncommon fine apples were sold at one shilling per peck, or one penny per pound.

Sunday October 26th 1788. Mr. Greenwood preached his first sermon in Oldham Church. Text, 2nd Corinthians, 13 Chaper 11 verse.

Radcliffe Betty, Miss, formerly of Foxdenton, but late of Manchester was buried at Oldham, November 12th 1788; disorder, a consumption, age 50 years.

Scofield Mary, daughter of John Scofield of Beartrees died November 9th 1788; disorder, a consumption age 29 years.

Page 26

November 13th 1788 one George Mellowdew was taken to the Sessions at Oldham by John Woolsoncroft, especial constable, Edmund Simpson (and) James Butterworth, overseers, to give Bond upon Bastardy but notwithstanding the vigilance of the Gentlemen of Chadderton he made a clear escape. (*4)

Walking match from Northmoor to Littlebrough, November 16th 1788, betwixt Abraham Taylor and a Yorkshireman. Won by the former. Time 1 hour 25 minutes.

Wood Thomas, son of Jenny Wood, died November 17th 1788, age 2 days.

Money lost by Michael Rowbottom, on the 9th of November 1788. There was 13 guineas and was found the same morning by two boys.

Page 28 (27 not included)

Hilton Daniel, Innkeeper of bottom of Greenacres Moor, died November 23rd 1788.

Daton James, joiner and carpenter, of Oldham died November 26th 1788.

Robbery. Thomas Creswell of Lees was robbed as he was going to Stockport Market of his purse containing 40 guineas by a single footpad. November 28th 1788.

Halkyard Jane, died at Oldham Workhouse December 4th 1788.

James Scofield of Bottom of Northmoor, had a cow, hanged herself in the shippen December 1788.

Some notorious villains cut a pear tree down belonging to James Clegg of Northmoor, December 6th 1788 and the following night some rogues stole a valuable box out of the house of Thomas Buckly of Beartrees.

Page 29

Travis, wife of John Travis of Oldham, grocer and chandler was buried at Shaw Chapel, December 11th 1788.

Ward John, butcher of Oldham died very suddenly December 15th 1788.

Fire: The factory belonging to Messrs Travis, Ogden & Kay situated at Shapashes was burned entirely to ashes; it was insured for £800, December 16th 1788.

Buckly, wife of John Buckly, yeoman, died December 20th 1788 at the house at Cowhill.

Ogden Isaac died at Chadderton Workhouse, December 24th 1788 aged 82.

Daughter of John Hardman, Innkeeper died of a mortification in her face, December 26th 1788 age 4 years.

1789, 1790 and 1791

The year '88 concluded with a severe frost and the New Year began the same. It froze with uncommon severity for upwards of 8 weeks. On the 13th January '89 it was an uncommon day for wind and snow that it was not safe for persons to stir out of doors. At night it happily turned to thawing when it was so uncommon slippery that a deal of persons had the misfortunes to break their limbs especially in Manchester where it was so slippery that people were skating in the very streets. It was proved that it has not froze so since the Great Storm 1789.

Ogden Jane, wife of Alexander Ogden of Burnley Lane died January 8th 1789; Disorder and palsey age 63.

Sarah, wife of Jonathan Dareding, Tailor of Oldham died January 21st 1789; disorder and fever.

Ashton James, of Wood died of a few days sickness January 28th 1789; disorder dry gripes age 34.

Thursday February 5th at the Sessions at Joseph Taylors, Sandylane, 4 weavers were ordered to the house of correction for embezelling their masters work.

Robberies: the house of one Whithead of Lane Ends near Denton was broke open and robbed of a sum of money betwixt the 5th and 6th of February 1789.

Barnes Nathen, Butcher of Oldham died after languishing one year and a half for about so long ago he lying drunk in the Highway was run over by a cart and both thighs broke. Died February 7th 1789.

Partington, wife of William Partington, bricklayer of Chadderton died suddenly, February 8th 1789.

Patten James of Chapelcroft was interred at Oldham, Feb 15th 1789.

Heanthorn Adam of Oldham was interred at Oldham Feb 16th 1789.

Woolstoncroft Jonathan, commonly called "Donty at Barn" was buried at Oldham, February 19th 1789.

Lingard Betty, of Leeshall buried at Oldham, February 24th 1789. She was a long time sorely afflicted with fits age nearly 18 years old.

Briarly John, tailor of Oldham interred March 6th 1789.

March 13th 1789, this day an uncommon cold day attended with a great wind and a deal of snow. It hath been very cold for several days past and like nothing but a cold bleak Spring.

Ogden John, of Chadderton-fold died after a tedious illness. March 31st 1789.

Neild Hannah, relect of the late John Neild, parish clerk and innkeeper died at Oldham April 1st 1789.

Haywood John, son of John Haywood of Maggott-lane died at an early age April 3rd 1789.

Thursday March 19th there was the greatest elumination and other demonstrations of joy in Oldham ever remembered and in other places the same on account of His Majesty's happy recovery from sickness (*5).

Chadderton Fold

Page 5

Scott Alice, wife of Joseph Scott, Hatter of Oldham died April 12th 1789.

A child of about 2 year old killed at bottom of Hollinwood by a cart belonging to Mr. John Clegg, Timberman of Oldham owing to the negligence of Ashworth the Driver, for which he was commited to Lancaster Castle (April 16th 1789) Imprisoned 6 months.

April 20th 1789, an otter hunt (*6) at bottom of Northmoor.

May 1st 1789, last night one Bradley of Hollinwood, being assaulted in his own house by a gang of "Mayers" (*7) he found a loaded gun and dangerously wounded one Whitehead.

Page 6

Son of John Newton, breadbaker of Ashton-under-Lyne (was) killed by a cartwheel falling on him as they were greasing it. May 2nd 1789 aged 7 years.

Whitehead John, commonly called "Old Pincher" of Stock-lane House was buried at Oldham, May 6th 1789.

Taylor, wife of George Taylor, shoemaker of Oldham died of a short sickness, May 14th 1789; disorder a spotted fever.

Ogden Joseph, of bottom of Northmoor, formerly of Dunsters died of a few days sickness, May 27th 1789 age 82.

Taylor Abraham, of Thorpe died June 10th 1789 aged 85.

Page 7

Wood Mary, wife of George Wood of Northmoor died after a tedious and long illness, June 14th 1789, age 62.

Garside James, formerly of Northmoor died at Oldham June 20th 1789; disorder a consumption.

June 20th 1789 was interred at Oldham wife of Charles Stott of Maggot-lane Ann, wife of John Ashton of Oldham.

June 12th 1789 at the Sessions at Joseph Taylor's, Jonathan Mellor was commited to prison for 3 months for keeping a warp and cotton above the statute time. A woman was commited for one year (for) having a Bastard child.

Page 8

Mellor Joseph, commonly called "Joseph of Peggys", shoemaker, died at Oldham June 30th 1789. Disorder, a violent fever.

July 1st 1789, a girl of Mark Buckley's of Bent, Oldham, coming down two pair of stairs with a child of Mark's upon its back, she missing a foot they both fell down. The child lived half an hour and the girl was much bruised.

A child of John Duckwork's of Cowhill was drowned in a tub with about 2 quarts of water in it. July 6th 1789 age 1 year and a half.

John Taylor, commonly called "Old John of Keverlow" fell down the cellar steps at the Swan Inn in Oldham July 6th and died the next day 1789.

Page 9

Wild James, of Hollinwood, formerly Sexton, was unfortunately crushed in a sandpit on Hollinwood, July 8th 1789. He recovered again.

Turner, Thomas, a "Tramping Tailor" was apprehended at Oldham for having two living wives. July 18th 1789.

July 22nd 1789, James Woolsoncroft for Bastardy was put in the new dungeon at Oldham, and being the first inhabitant of this dreary mansion, received the charities of a gazing multitude.

July 22nd 1789 Two most tremendous cracks of thunder accompanied with vivid flashes of lightning, and it rained so excessively that the waters rose astonishingly.

July 22nd 1789, the body of Jackson, son of Henry Jackson, painter of Oldham was brought back to Oldham in a hearse, he having the misfortune to be killed at the Duke's Cut (*8) the night last.

View of Barton Bridge on the Bridgewater Canal, "The Duke's Cut"

Page 10

A girl of Bob Knot's of Holebottom was unfortunately drowned at Holebottom in Oldham, August 2nd 1789. Age betwixt 8 and 9.

Mr. Whitaker Samuel, chandler and grocer (of) Oldham died at Oldham, August 11th 1789.

August 2nd 1789 this Summer has been an uncommon wet one, particularly the last 7 weeks, it having rained uncommonly most of the time through which the Markets of provisions rose uncommonly high.

Ingham, John of Priest-hill Oldham, being intoxicated, fell upon the ground and immediately died, September 1st 1789.

Wednesday, September 2nd 1789, there was a meeting of the Freemasons at Oldham when the Reverend Mr. Wrigly preached before them from Romans 13, Chapter 10 verse.

Ashton Joseph, of Cowhill, died of a few days sickness, September 2nd 1789.

Clegg, John, the younger Timber merchant of Oldham was unfortunately drowned at Liverpool whilst bathing, September 3rd 1789. He was buried at Blakeley. The text of his funeral was Deuteronomy 33 chap 29 verse.

A lamentable misfortune on Thursday September 17th 1789 as Abraham Ingram and William Carr were drawing some old carbs out of an old coalpit at Alkrington. The pit suddenly closed up and took down with it the headstocks and Richard Ramsden, the overlooker of the works, and enclosed them all in one grave.

It was impossible to come at the dead bodies as the pit was nearly full of water so that their bodies will never be found. Ramsden left a wife and 12 children. Carr, a wife and three children and her pregnant. Ingham was married about a month ago and left a wife and another woman big with child.

Lord Charles of Uinn Nook, died after a painful and tedious illness, October 1st 1789. Disorder, a consumption.

A most tremendous fire broke out at the Staffordshire Warehouse at the Duke's Cut, Manchester, which burnt totally to the ground. The damage supposed to be £5000. Not insured for one penny - October 1st 1789.

Ogden, Dinah, wife of John Ogden of Dry Clough, formerly Keeper of the Red Lion Inn in Royton, died October 19th 1789.

Johnson George, joiner of Dolstile, died October 23rd 1789. Disorder, a fever.

Hall James, of Uinn Nook, an old pensioner died in an advanced age. October 30th 1789.

Mills John, of Hollinwood, a celebrated mechanic, died October 31st 1789.

Mrs. Goodwin, relict of the late Mr. Goodwin, Excise Officer, Oldham, died October 29th 1789.

Brierley Betty, wife of John Brierley, badger, Oldham died in the prime of life of a spotted fever. November 2nd 1789.

Mr. Thomas Hobson of Oldham died November 24th 1789.

Ogden, John, formerly keeper of the Red Lion, Royton died at Alderoot, November 30th 1789. Disorder, apoplexy, age 64.

December 5th 1789, Mally Heighs and Sally her daughter died this day of a violent fever which raged at this time.

Winterbottom Josuah, of Oldham, Cotton Manufacturer, died December 6th 1789.

Molly, wife of Js. Rowbottom, Innkeeper, Alderoot, died December 21st 1789, age 27 years.

It should have been remarked in its proper place that Damson plums in October 1789 sold at 3 halfpence per Quart. In 1788, they sold at 5 pence per Quart.

The year 1789 concluded with uncommon wet weather and the year 1790 begun with the same.

1790

On January 1st and 2nd 1790, died the following persons viz:-

James Potter of Dollstile, a pensioner of Chelsea Hospital.

Joseph Lees, formerly an eminent Shoemaker, age 85 years, at Oldham.

Richard Sylvio, a tailor of Oldham, who buried his wife about 3 weeks ago. They both died of a Fever.

Betty Bamford of Bent, of a Fever.

A daughter of James Wilds, Barber of Oldham, of a Fever.

George Chadderton, Collier, of Oldham, died January 17th 1790 of a Fever.

Page 16

Philip Brickly, Collier of Oldham. It was a false report of Philip's death.

And Christopher Mawood, tailor of Oldham, died January 22nd 1790. Disorder, a Fever.

Betty, wife of the above Philip Brickly, died about a fortnight ago of a Fever.

John Whittaker, Keeper of the Hare and Hounds Inn in Oldham, died January 27th 1790 and wife of Abraham Jackson, commonly called "Slandering" of Oldham died January 27th 1790.

Hannah, wife of Henry Harrison, Clogger, died of a Fever, January 29th 1790.

Page 17

Sacrilege.

On Thursday night, the 28th January 1790, the Chapel of Newton Heath was broken open and stripped of some articles, but the communion plate was not within which missed them of their booty. Also the same night, the Chapel on Hollinwood was broke open and robbed of the pulpit cushion and the Communion Cloth torn and mostly taken away. The plate was not within.

James Mills of Northmoor died February 4th 1790. Disorder, a Fever; same day died.

James Halliwell of Oldham. Disorder a Fever.

Thomas Skellet, a Yorkshireman, died of a fever at Oldham. February 5th 1790.

Betty Winterbottom of Red Lion, Oldham, died February 12th 1790; a consumption.

Page 18

Joseph Ogden of Maggot-lane died February 21st 1790 age 65. Disorder, dry gripes. He, at an early age entered himself into the army in the 23rd Regiment, was in the Battle of Dettingen (*9) and continued in the army (for) that war and the war following. He was entrusted with service which he ever fulfilled with the greatest integrity and honour.

John Sidebottom died at Chadderton, February 20th 1790. He was aged 16 years. Disorder, a fever.

George Cook, joiner of Fog Lane died February 23rd 1790. Age 48 years. Disorder; a dropsey.

During a fit of sickness which I was attacked with the following persons died (which lasted from February 17th to April 18th) viz:-

Page 19

Susan Mills of Oldham, a fever.

John Brearly Badger of Oldham, whose wife died in November last; a fever.

A daugher of Tom Cleggs of Oldham, Hatter, a fever.

Anna, daughter of John Chadwick of Mumps, of a fever.

Ann, daughter of Isaac Clegg of Mumps, of a fever.

Widow of the late John Taylor of Cockhouse-fold of a fever. Both died March 19th 1790.

Thomas, son of John Mills of Maggot-lane died March 22nd 1790. Disorder a consumption.

March 24th, James Barclay, commonly called "Little Man" was buried at Oldham.

Martha Mills, an elderly woman died at Oldham, March 26th 1790. Disorder a fever.

Edmund Rogers died at Scholesfold March 26th 1790. Disorder a fever.

Edmund Heap, Master of the Crown and Cushion Inn died March 26th 1790, disorder a consumption.

March 29th, a girl of William Beswick's near Cowhill burned so much that it died on the 31st.

Wife of Peter Platt died April 6th 1790 of a fever.

On Thursday April 9th 1790, Miss Mary Horton, sister to the late Sir William Horton Bart, was interred at Oldham.

April 10th 1790. Edmund Ogden and John Heys of Northmoor were conveyed to a House of Correction at Manchester to take their trials for stealing a woman's petticoat.

John Marler of Chadderton Mill died of a fever, April 11th 1790.

April 10th 1790. A most tremendous high wind which did great damage to buildings and at Joseph Pickford's of Royton it blew down 2 large chimneys which broke the roof and all the floors into the cellar and the family miraculously escaped death.

Mary, wife of Thomas Ogden of Busk died April 16th 1790.

March 5th 1790, Robert Wrigley entered as a tenant to the Red Lion Inn Oldham.

James Mills, ringer of the Great Bell at Oldham was buried April 24th 1790; disorder a fever.

Wife of the late Thomas Hobson, Mercer & Draper Oldham, died April 23rd 1790.

April 29th 1790 being Ashton Fair a gang of pickpockets were detected and the day following were brought before Joseph Pickford Esquire of Royton when one was committed and 6 discharged.

Phinias Neild, keeper of the Anchor Inn Oldham died May 1st 1790.

Edmund Whitehead of Coldhurst Lane died May 2nd 1790.

Jonathan Neild of Oldham died in an advanced age, April 30th 1790. He was formerly a man of property. Died poor.

May 7th 1790. Last night a man fell into the Engine pit at Werneth and was killed on the spot. (He was a collier belonging to these pits).

Grace, wife of James Neild, Innkeeper in Oldham died May 14th 1790.

John Jackson, commonly called "John of Ralphs", died at Oldham May 31st 1790.

A son of Joseph Wild's, Carter in Nathan-row Oldham unfortunately drowned, June 1st 1790, age 3 years.

June 11th 1790. This day there was a sale of the property of William Booth, late of Royton, when the house late acquired by Joseph Taylor was sold to James Franklin for £259. The meadow and two cottages for 220 pounds to William Schofield. The factory for something under £500 to one Kenyon. They were situated near Street Bridge.

Sarah, wife of John Hardman, Innkeeper of Oldham, died June 14th 1790. She was own sister to John Hardman's last wife.

Mr. Richard Bury of Royley buried June 6th 1790.

William Winterbottom died at Oldham of a consumption, June 17th 1790.

John Shaw, formerly of Beartrees died near Chadderton, July 5th 1790.

Ann Newton died after being afflicted for 6 years. July 7th 1790. She died at Bent, age 28 years.

July 26th 1790. This day there was a concert of music at Blackridings near Cowhill.

August 9th 1790 there was a coiting at Northmoor betwixt John Hilton of Greenacres Moor and John Wild the celebrated footman, which was won by the former.

A son of Steward Smedhurst's of Bent, Oldham, unfortunately killed by the tailpole belonging to Carding Robin at Bent, Oldham. August 23rd 1790 age about 6 years.

John Dean was executed at Chester for the murder of his wife, September 2nd 1790 and the day following was hung in chains on Stockport Moor.

James M. Namara was executed on Kersal Moor for burglary. September 11th 1790.

A boy of 9 years of age was killed at Royley Coalpits, September 10th 1790.

Mary, wife of Michael Rowbottom died September 15th 1790 age 58 years.

Betty, wife of James Butterworth of Nodd died September 20th 1790. Disorder, a violent fever.

September 27th 1790. Edward Barlow opened his Public House in Maggot-lane for the first time and to grace it like other Alehouses there was uncommon fighting.

September 27th 1790 Damson plums sold for 8 pence to 9 pence per Quart.

October 20th 1790, this being the yearly Feast of the Sick Clubs, Mr. Fawcett preached from the 2nd Book of Thessilonians, 3 Chapter, 10th verse.

Sunday October 24th 1790, as some Colliers were blasting an old stock of wood at Cowhill, Betty Howard imprudently standing too near, a splinter flew from the stock and stuck in the back part of her head and most dangerously wounded her.

November 4th 1790, a child of John Wooley's, bricklayer of Chadderton so miserably burnt that in a few days it died.

John Scofield, alias "John Jonas" of Boggart Hole died November 23rd 1790.

November 24th 1790, a mare belonging to one John Standering at Shaw Chapel trotted from Oldham to Manchester, nearly 7 miles in 28 minutes 58½ seconds for 6 guineas. The owner rode her and was allowed . . .

. . . 32 minutes. The mare was not 13 hands high and was Broken, Winded and in foal.

James Ogden, shoemaker of Busk died November 25th 1790. Age 37 years.

November 26th 1790 this day Captain Charles Pickford's Independent Company marched through Oldham on their way to Chatham.

George Worthington of Chadderton, formerly a Walkmiller (*10) died December 4th 1790.

Thomas Horton of Holroyd Esquires had a son baptised at Chadderton Hall called Josuah Thomas.

Mrs. Sally Horton, sister to the late Sir William Horton, Bart, buried at Oldham. December 10th 1790.

A daughter of John Binns, Collier of Goldbourn unfortunately drowned at Shapashes, December 13th 1790. Age 9 years.

Greenaces, December 9th 1790. Last night one Charles Williamson broke into the house of Richard Waring of Greenacres and stole out a silver watch, two bills of Exchange and a quantity of gold and silver. He was taken the day following to Stockport. He had broke out of Chelsea jail where he had been commited for house breaking.

Abraham Cocker of Heighside, formerly of Wood, was intered Oldham, December 17th 1790.

Walk Mill, Chadderton

Page 30

Ralph Collier of Royton, committed to the New Bailey for security, he having a woman with child, December 16th 1790. His age upwards of 70 years.

Betty Marshall, formerly Betty Atherton, interred at Oldham, December 13th 1790.

December 15th 1790, last night the wind rose astonishingly and unrooted a deal of helpless thatched cots. It likewise blew down a large factory in Manchester. The bricks fell upon a cottage near it wherein was a child of 6 years old, a man and his wife. The child was killed dead, the man and his wife much bruised.

December 23rd 1790. Last night it was uncommon stormy and wind very high which unroofed a deal of thatched houses. Very loud cracks of thunder and vivid flashes of lightning.

Cash Gate Cottage, the last thatched cottage in Oldham

Page 31

A lamentable misfortune on the 21st December 1790. A large Cotton Factory in Hanover Street, Manchester suddenly fell down about 11 o'clock, forenoon, when the people were at work. 3 were killed and (a) great number miserably hurt besides a number of horses killed and wounded. Its falling was attributed to the springing of an arch in one of the cellars under it. 2 have died of their wounds.

Betty, wife of Robert Woolsoncroft of Couldhurst, High Barn, died December 27th 1790. Disorder, a consumption age 38.

John Andrew of Old Clarks, died December 30th 1790 age 80 years.

Ann Ashton, servant at the Packhorse, Failsworth, died suddenly. December 30th 1790.

1791

January 1st. John Buckly summoned before Joseph Pickford Esq for defrauding John Clegg of one cow's head.

John Jackson, commonly called "Nooker" died January 3rd.

January 8th. Last night an uncommon windy night, the wind blew with uncommon rapidity and a great deal of thunder and lightning.

Robert Jackson Badger of Oldham died January 8th.

January 11th, coals uncommon scarce, particularly in Manchester where they are sold at 8 pence per basket.

Several poor families subsisting nearly without coals. It is owing to the gentlemen of Manchester having a dispute with the Duke of Bridgewater.

Hatting

On the 14th of January the cotton, in drying at Edmund Mellors, Top o'th'Moor caught fire and consumed about 7 ponds together with the flake, a silk handerchief, one volume of the Newgate Calendar was materially damaged.

January 17th, this night uncommon loud cracks of thunder attended with great flashes of lightning.

Hanna, wife of John Ogden, innkeeper ("Unicorn") Royton, died January 18th. Disorder, a consumption.

Page 3

James Lees, Fustian maker of Broadway Lane died January 23rd; disorder dry gripes.

Bad effects of Guns

January 24. This morning James Garside of Royton, in discharging a loaded gun, the breech pin flew out and stuck in his forehead. Immediate assistance was obtained but notwithstanding he died on the 28th, age 21 years.

Very few family's where guns are generally used escape without some dreadful misfortune.

James Starkey, Esquire of Heywood near Bury, High Sheriff for 1791.

Samuel Cheetham, commonly called "Sam Sowl Poak" died about February 1791 in Oldham Workhouse.

Page 4

Alice Greaves of Oldham, died February 18th age 89.

May, wife of James Crompton, Hatter, Oldham died February 18th; disorder a consumption age 35.

February 1791, beef sells at 5 pence per pound, Mutton 5 pence, Pork 5 pence, Veal 5 pence, meal 1s 7d per peck; treacle 3d per lb, old butter 8d, new butter 9d per lb, bacon 8d.

Mary, wife of James Clegg of Northmoor died March, 2 day. Disorder, a dropsey. Age 74 years.

A male child of John Jackson's of Maggot Lane, unfortunately drowned March 8th, age 2 years.

Page 5

Mary, wife of John Mills of Maggot Lane died March 12th. Disorder, a consumption.

James Hartley, a collier was killed at Werneth Coalpits, March 22nd.

Ralph Barnes of Doabhouse died suddenly March 23rd, a great age.

Onions sold 4 pence per pound in March this year.

Oldham, March 28th, last night the factory belonging to James Smethurst was broke open and a large quantity of cotton stolen.

Richard Banks was so burned by the Firey damp at Werneth that he died a few days after. March 21st.

Page 6

Mark Buckley, shoemaker, but late a spinner, died suddenly at Oldham April 5th.

Sarah, wife of Abraham Crompton, Chapel Croft, Oldham died April 16th.

Old Alice Hellawell of Churchyard, buried at Oldham, April 26.

The house of John Stockton, Mule spinner of Blakeley Street, Manchester, got on fire. His wife and 4 children were burnt to atoms. The husband wife's sister, 2 children escaped out at the windows though their limbs broke and much bruised. April 30th.

A girl, 3 years old, of William Whittaker's of Top'O'the Moor so miserably burned by her clothes taking fire that she died the next day, May 1st.

Page 7

Jane, relect of the late Weedall, late of Couldhurst, Highbarn buried at Oldham May 18th.

Wife of John Lingat of Leeshall died of a violent fever, May 16th.

May 14th. New potatoes sold in Oldham 4 pence per pound.

The large ox, the first prize at the Welch Main won by Tom Shallcross and Co, arrived at Oldham and inspected by the public at 2d per piece. May 14th.

James Walton, alias "Wrangle", for an assault on Sarah Gibbins, commited to the New Bailey, May 17th.

Page 8

We must observe that last winter was an uncommon mild one, even opener than the winter before; this spring one of the earliest ever known till May, when it turned to uncommon cold till the 26th, when it made the appearance of a fine summer.

2 Streetbridge colliers for breaking the house of Edmund Taylor of Thornham Lane, commited to Lancaster to take their trials, by Joseph Pickford, May 20th.

Joseph Wild of Nathan Row, much burned by a quantity of gunpowder taking fire, May 26th.

Nathan Robinson's galloway, from Oldham to Wakefield, May 31st.

Sarah Mills of Rettom Nook, died June 2nd. Disorder, a consumption.

Page 9

John Cocker of Netherhouse, Crompton, in a fit of insanity cut his belly open, June 8th and died June 10th.

June 12th, uncommon hot for about a fortnight last, when it changed to severe cold so that it froze severely and the neighbouring hills were covered with snow.

Wife of Ralph Mellor of Northmoor died July 9th, Disorder a fever.

Two children of James Mellors, Smith Edge lane, died of a fever about the beginning of July.

June 14th. It froze astonishingly this morning.

Page 10

Betty, wife of John Buckley of Busk died July 11th age 68.

John Chadwick Badger of Oldham died July 12th.

Wife of Richard Linsey, weaver, of Royton delivered of 3 children, July 13th, who with the mother are doing well.

John Ogden of Busk commited to the New Bailey, July 6th for fishing in the grounds of Mr. Hopwood of Hopwood.

Thomas, his son, committed for same offence to the above prison July 12th

James Hardman of Oldham died July 15th. Disorder; a pleursey fever. A man very eminent in music.

Page 11

July 17th, an uncommon hot day, the heat nearly unsupportable. Has been very hot for several days attended with uncommon falls of honey so that the leaves of the oak were cemented together.

July 20th, John & Thomas Ogden liberated from the New Bailey on condition of paying ten pounds for fishing.

Sian Buckley, son of Ben Buckley of Chadderton Heights, died July 23rd in the prime of life. Disorder; a consumption.

July 25th, at the conclusion of the Quarter Sessions, James Walton was discharged, Gibbins having brought no Bill (See page 7).

Page 12

July 14th, a most dangerous riot broke out at Birmingham owing to some gentlemen celebrating The French Revolution. It was celebrated in Manchester, London and most of great towns on the above day. (*11)

July 26, the Bishop of Chester held a confirmation at Manchester for that town and the neighbouring parishes and confirmed 2368 males and 2968 females. In all 5336 souls.

July 27, the Bishop of Chester confirmed at Rochdale 3000 and upwards. Owing to the crowding, one of the Gallerys gave way whereby one girl was killed.

August 2nd, Richard Hornby, clockmaker and hardware man died in an advanced age.

August 4th bilberrys sold at Oldham, 5 pence per quart owing to failure in the crops owing to the frosts which destroyed the blossom.

Page 13

July 7th. Mr. Pickford, carrier from Manchester obtained a verdict of £200 against W. Jawlett of Stony Stafford for having reported that he was become bankrupt.

A most dangerous riot at Sheffield owing to enclosing some commons or wastelands, July 16th (*12).

A lamentable misfortune. Benjamin Woolstoncroft, carter to Mr. John Cleggs, Bart, returning from Manchester had the misfortune to fall off his cart which was loaded with wool. The wheel going over his body he died the next morning, August 13th.

> "The fortunate have years
>   And those they choose
>   The unfortunate have days
>   And those they loose"

Page 14

August 16th, uncommon hot for some days past and last night loud cracks of thunder with vivid flashes of lightning and a cow of Sir W. Horton Bart's killed in the park thereby.

August 16th, a scaffold at the New factory, Stock Lane, broke down whereby some of the workmen were much bruised.

August 19th, last night died at Oldham George Scholes, long time servant to Mr. Whittaker, Chandler, Oldham. Disorder: a dropsey.

August 28th, being Oldham Rush-bearing Sunday, it was an uncommon wet day and very few strangers attended.

On Wednesday, August 31st, a wetter day was seldom seen.

Sir Watts Horton (1753-1811)

John Smethurst, a man famous in casting waters died at Oldham August 29th.

Page 15

August 7th, the two houses late property of Mr. Hornby Oldham were sold by auction and bought by Thomas Ogden, Failsworth for Mr. John Wright. The sum £910.

August 5th. Some villains broke into the house of the late George Scholes and stole 4 guineas and a half at Oldham.

September 9th. The Assizes ended at Lancaster when James Silcock and James Ashurst the two Streetbridge colliers were acquitted (See page 8).

Page 16

September 7th, the two houses late Mr. Hornby's, Oldham were sold by auction.

Sept 15th the mail was robbed and the boy inhumanely murdered betwixt Manchester and Warrington and no traces left to discover the offenders.

Sept 19th. The Bull Bait (*13) the New Bailey, Maggott Lane.

September 26th. A boy about 9 years old, his hand blown off and miserably torn and bruised by a powder horn taking fire in his hand by imprudently trailing some on the fire at a coalpit. Caught fire near Little Green.

Uncommon fine weather for 2 months past and has been hotter than was ever known at this time. October 7th.

Page 17

New market at Middleton. September 30th the first market commenced and owing to the fineness of the day was uncommonly crowded. Meal sold 32s per load, flour 34s, potatoes 5d and 6d, cheese 5d per lb and old butter 8½d, mutton 4d per lb, beef 4d, apples 2d per peck, damson plums 6d per quart.

A man painting top of Ashton Church (inside) had the misfortune to fall and was killed. October 1st.

John Smith, a Yorkshireman, killed in a Sinking Pit in Sour Road Oldham by a large stone falling on him. October 8th.

Page 18

October 1st. This day Charles Williamson for Burglary in the dwelling house of Richard Waring at Greenacres (see page 29 for 1790) was executed at Lancaster.

Walking Match

James Pearson, for a wager of 20 guineas walked from Manchester to Middleton and back (12 miles), in 30 seconds under 2 hours. 2 hours was the given time.

October 19th, being the yearly feast of the Sick Clubs, Oldham, Mr. Fawcett preached from 2nd Book of Thessilonians, 3rd Chapter, 10th verse.

On Sunday, October 23rd, T. Buckley, T. Ogden and B. Ogden of Northmoor took up a buck and sold him to Mr. Pickford for £1 2s.

Page 19

John Brearly Taylor of Chapel Croft Oldham died in a fit of apoplexy October 28th.

Betty, wife of John Taylor of Broughton, formerly of Northmoor died November 1st.

Uncommon crops of potatoes this season so that they were uncommon plentiful. Sold from 5 to 6 shillings per load.

Mary Nicholls, formerly an innkeeper in Oldham died at a great age, November 2nd.

November 6th. This day 6 pound of cotton burnt by accidently catching fire at our own house.

Charles Schofield of Alderroot, formerly in the Manchester Volunteers died November 9th. Disorder; a consumption.

Page 20

James Fitton of Hopkinfold died at Greenacres Moor in a fit of apoplexy, November 11th.

One Moors of Alkrington returning home with a cart and riding therein the horses drew to near a stand of water. The cart flew over and Moors found drowned and the horses nearly starved to death. November 12th.

November 19th and 20th. Two uncommon wet windy days. The waters rose so high in Saddleworth that near Woods a bridge was washed away and a young man passing over was drowned and his body not found.

November 19th. This day one Hall, for a trifling wager, undertook to go from Stalybridge to a mill about 1 mile and a half off during the storm this day and through the severity of the cold, dropped down and died immediately.

November 23rd. Last night some rogues broke into the house of Mr. Hopwood of Hopwood and stole a quantity of wearing apparel and got off undiscovered.

December 4th, died at Hollinwood, Mrs. Worthington, relect of the late Mr. George Worthington of Werneth.

Betty, wife of John Collins of Hollinwood interred December 20th; disorder a fever.

Wife of James Graves, tailor of Chadderton, died December 25th. Disorder, a fever.

James Hulme discharged for want of evidence, he having been charged with stealing 20 warps from Mr. Rowbottom, December 26th.

This year concluded with a severe frost and deep snow but about the last day turned to thawing.

FINIS

1792

The New Year commenced this year on Sunday which was a fine thawing day. Owing to the flourishing of all sorts of trades there was plenty of Christmas fair necessaries of every sort. Excessive dear, particularly sugar and coals.

	s.	d.	
Malt	1	7½	per pk
Meal	1	8	per pk
Very fine flour	1	10	per pk
Cheese	0	5	per pound
New butter	0	10	per pound
Old butter	0	8	per pound
Treacle	0	4	per pound
Brown Sugar	0	10	per pound
Pork	0	5	per pound
Beef	0	5	per pound
Mutton	0	5	per pound
Potatoes	5	6	per load
Coals	0	10	down at the pit

Mary, relict of the late James Hardman died suddenly at Oldham, January 2nd.

January 6th, this day Mr. Jacob Radcliffe, hatter, Oldham made a grand feast and the guests were selected from the most indigent widows and widowers and old men and their wives. (When) they sat down to a very good supper and plenty of ale which afforded them a great relief at this inclement time of the year which reflects the greatest honour on their noble donor.

The Strangers Friends Society (*14) at Manchester instituted this Christmas for relieving persons they found of all religions and nations in distressed circumstances at Manchester.

January 11th, Thomas Whittaker and William Jackson, constables of Oldham took into custody 36 strollers (*15) before Mr Pickford of Royton when most of them were passed to their settlements.

During the year 1791, there were in Manchester 1300 marriages and from the 1st to the 5th January 1792 there were 58 marriages and 56 baptisms.

During the 10th, 11th, 12th and 13th of January it froze so uncommonly hard as hardly to be equalled in the annals of freezing. It is worthy of remark it was exceedingly calm.

James Ashton of Cowhill who died in an advanced age was interred at Oldham January 26th.

January 26th, this day Sir Wallis Horton Bart, Lady Horton and Miss Horton with a large retinue left Chadderton Hall for London. (*16)

John, son of David Wolstoncroft of Whittaker Fold died at Clifton very suddenly. It was surmised that he had been wounded in a conflict said to have happened at Swinton, but upon the matter being fully investigated, it appeared that there had been no blows, but that he had been put into violent passions which brought on a fever. He was ill about 40 hours. Age 18 years, January 25th.

James Hilton, tailor, formerly of Hunt-lane was interred at Middleton February 5th. He was buried in his stockings, breeches, waistcoat, shirt and neckcloth and coat (at his own request).

February 9th, this day a person in the character of a rider was detected at Abraham Fletchers,

Werneth, passing off base silver coin and taken before Joseph Pickford of Royton and by him commited to the New Bailey.

February 9th. A boy servant to James Hill of Newton Heath, on mounting a horse at Werneth coalpits, the beast turned restive and run backwards into a coalpit with the boy on his back. The horse was dashed to pieces. The boy was found still mounted with his thigh much broke but likely to do well - the pit measures 106 yards deep.

William Asheton of Curedale, High Sheriff for 1792.

Page 6

James Lees, commonly called 'James of Margarets' killed by a cartwheel going over his head. He accidentally fell as he was walking on the road on Hollinwood being much drunk. He was a hatter and lived in Oldham? February 21.

Ralph Jackson, Parish Clerk of Oldham, died February 20th. Disorder, a consumption. He was elected Clerk on Oldham Rushbearing Wednesday in 1782. (The text at his funeral, all Isaiah 26, Chp. 4, verse 9).

Nanny Lee of Chadderton Lane died at a great age and interred February 22nd. February 19th, being Shrove Sunday, and on Monday and Tuesday there were married at Manchester 58 couples.

Page 7

Edward Hide, Master of the Cock alehouse in Tonge, died February 26th, disorder, consumption. Age 48 years.

Murder

February 20th, in consequence of some altercation betwixt John Whitehead of Hollinwood and Ralph Rutter, a collier, Rutter without much provocation struck Whitehead a little above his ear and burst a blood vessel so that he languished until the 24th and then died. Rutter was committed to the New Bailey until Whitehead's death and on the Jury bringing in their verdict of 'Wilful Murder' he was of consequence committed to Lancaster Castle. This affair happened at Werneth.

Sian Partington of Oldham interred February 29th, and morning following his wife expired. Disorders, consumption.

Page 8

John Taylor of Foul leach fell into a sawpit (being much intoxicated). He lay most part of the night of the 12th February and languished until the 26th and then died.

Joseph Hall of Oldham committed to the New Bailey to take his trial for stealing 5s & 6d out of the house of Chadderton Oldham.

This Hall was tried and convicted last October Sessions for stealing a pair of shoes from Mr. Clegg, Timber Merchant. Committed March 2nd.

Martha, wife of Joshua Kershaw of Top o'th' Moor died in an advanced age, March 5th.

James Butterworth of Nod, died March 6th, disorder pleurasy fever age 57. N.B. This James Butterworth was married, February 19th last past.

Page 9

March 6th. Last night the New Bailey Alehouse on Fire but happily got under without much damage.

March 10th, this day the Assizes began at Lancaster when Ralph Rutter, charged with the murder of John Whitehead (see page 7) was found guilty of Manslaughter. Sentence, fined 1 shilling and 3 month's imprisonment.

At the above Assizes, it was supposed that Daniel Murphy, the person supposed to have murdered Mr.Worthington in 1788 would have been tried but Mr. Butterworth could not obtain him from the Jailor in Dublin, he being detained on account of a highway robbery.

March 20th. Last night died in an advanced age, Mrs. Taylor of Thorp whose death was mentioned by mistake (in page 9).

Betty, wife of Sam Duerdin of Chapelcroft, Oldham interred March 26th.

March 25th, this day a child of Thomas Johnsons of Chadderton Mill fell into the brook near the Mill and the water being high, the stream carried it down to Chadderton Green where it was picked out of the water with little hopes of life, but by using the means recommended by the Humane Society, it was happily brought to life.

April 1st, last night an uncommon rainy, boisterous night.

Chadderton, March 22nd, this day a new-born infant male child was found floating in the brook here. Upon the Coronor taking an inquest on the body, it appeared that the said child was born of the body of Mary Greathead of Chadderton, but late of Bedale, Yorkshire, on the night of the 17th instant, and was thrown into the brook by one Grace Stansfield at the request of its mother. It appeared that Stansfield was requested to empty a chamber pot into the water and she, ignorant of its contents obeyed the order. A verdict was found against Greathead of Wilful Murder. She was, of course, fully committed to Lancaster Castle but first she was to lay in 'til she was able to undertake the journey.

Hay sold this spring at one shilling per stone and onions 3 pence per pound.

April 12th, an otter baited at Joel's Dam.

April 9th, being Easter Monday, the celebrated Stump run two races on Kersall Moor, one mile each and within one hour of each other. The first race he beat Matthew Chapman - one full mile; time 4 mins 47 seconds. The second he beat Thomas Seddon, one full mile and notwithstanding they were several times annoyed with the crowd particularly Seddon. They run it in 4 mins 49 seconds. Seddon's party dispute losing and the wager is yet in dispute. It was afterwards agreed to have each their own money.

On same day. James Kennion of Bury beat Robert Booth of Radclyffe Bridge 4 miles, time 22 minutes.

March 29th, this day Gustavus, King of Sweden died of the wounds he received from the discharge of a pistol. He being a tyrant and an enemy to LIBERTY was murdered by the hands of one of his own Courtiers.

Mottos:

E. Derby's	"Without changing"
Lord Grey de Wilton	"I trust to virtue, nor force"
Lord Byron	"Trust Byron"
E. Fitzwilliam	"Let your desires obey your reason".

Grosvenors:	"Virtue, not pedigree is the mark of Nobility"

Earl Derby, born Sept. 1752.

Lord Stanley, born April 21st 1775.

Mrs. Elizabeth Horton, born 1748, married July 28 1779 to Thomas Horton.

Mrs. Lucy Hornby, born 1750, married April 25th 1778.

Harriot, born 1756, married Sir W. Horton, June 3rd 1778.

Chadderton Hall, April 24th. This day arrived Sir Watts and Lady Horton Bart. A pity that the prevailing fashion and superfluety of dress should so much attract the attention of females as to cause them . . .

. . . to shrink from the paths of virtue and respectability. Such has been the weakness of Susan Lord of Northmoor who was this day found to have robbed her late Master, John Mellor of Northmoor, April 24th.

Ann, daughter of Ralph Mellor of Northmoor, died April 25. Disorder, a consumption.

Oldham, April 21st, this day mutton sold 5 pence halfpenny, and 6 pence per pound, beef and veal in proportion.

May 1st day, a very severe cold day and severe hailstorms.

April 28th at the conclusion of Manchester Sessions . . .

. . . Joseph Hall for stealing money out of Chadderton's house (see page 8), he was only 14 years old, was imprisoned for 2 years in the New Bailey prison.

March 24th. This day Werneth Hall with all its apartunances and Royalties were sold to Mr. Sidebottom and Co. of London for £24,500 and thought exceeding cheap.

Knutsford, May 1st. This day Thomas Hilton of Oldham beat Smith of Failsworth 140 yards for 50 guineas each. Bets 5 to 4 on the winner.

Busk, May 5th, this day arrived Philip Buckley, late of the Oxford Blues.

May 10th, this day the body of the young man who was drowned in November last, as mentioned on page 20 in last volume, was found buried in wreck near Mosley. We hear his name was T. Mills.

May 12th, died Robert Wrigley, Keeper of the Red Lion Inn, Oldham.

Mary Greathead was conveyed to Lancaster upon the charge of murder (see page 11) on the 12th May.

The month of May 1792 was uncommon wet and cold.

May 19th, this day Thomas Garlick of Block Lane had his cart robbed of goods to the value of £80 about midday during his being absent about 7 minutes.

William, son of Samuel Winterbottom, collier of Oldham, going with his father's dinner into a brest eye the roof fell and crushed him in such a shocking manner that his life is despaired of, May 19th.

George, commonly called "Longbutter" committed to the New Bailey for robbing a tramping woman near Stock-lane a few days since. May 25th.

May 28th. Last night died Elizabeth, wife of Thomas Hide of Chadderton. Disorder a consumption.

May 26th. Certain intelligence was received and the account was published in the Manchester newspapers etc. and the account signed by T.B.Bailey Esq. that Daniel Murphy was executed at Wicklow in Ireland, and that he confessed he murdered the late Mr. Worthington of Werneth.

June 9th, this day James Bloomley of Burnley Lane, imprudently riding upon one of the beams at Fairbottom had the misfortune to be very much bruised.

June 12th, this morning James Mellor of Cockhousefold, Oldham died. He had the misfortune on the 31st May last to fall and splinter his hipbone which brought on another disorder and put a period to his misery, age 60. He was a fustian manufacturer, but character contrary to most for he was sincerely a good man. (*17)

Engine at Fairbottom Bobs

During the months of March, April, May and June, Charity Sermons were preached in all churches and chapels of all religions for the use of Infirmary Manchester.

June 21st, died John Whitehead of Mill-lane End, Chadderton, far advanced in years. Disorder a pleuresy fever.

Page 21

June 22nd, this day was interred at Oldham wife of John Mill of Higginshaw and William Berry of Back o'th'Edge who died of a fever.

His Majesty's Proclamation against seditious publications was read by Ministers in their respective places of worship in the month of June.

A riot at Manchester June 4th, but little damage except pulling up a few innocent trees which grew in the Square and impiously placing them at the Dissenters' Chapels.

Page 22

June 29th, this day the Countinghouse of Mr. John Lees, Church Lane, Oldham was found to have been robbed of about £3 worth of copper coin and one Jones and one Haigh were found to have committed this robbery but upon their parents making up the money, the matter was dropped.

July 3rd at Kersal Moor, this day Thomas Seddon beat Abraham Kershaw commonly called "Loam Barn Lad" 4 miles for 50 guineas. Each time 20 minutes 39 seconds.

May 30th, Mr. Holt's scheme of converting the road from before Chadderton Hall lost by a great majority.

Page 23

July 9th. The Exchange at Manchester was sold by Public Auction to Messrs. Upton & Sons for £425 and their workmen began taking it down on Wednesday following.

Knutsford, July 16th, this day Fenton of Manchester beat Thomas Hilton of Oldham, 140 yards. Hilton gave Fenton 4 yards at starting. Fenton came in first, 3 yards at starting. High odds on winner.

July 15th. Uncommon loud cracks of thunder accompanied with vivid flashes of lightning attended with uncommon raining began early this morning at about 7 o'clock. A cow of John Street's of Grinbees was killed by lightning.

July 26th James Maddocks of Royton, Banksman, in doing his work at a coalpit, Royley, had the misfortune to fall down and (was) killed on the spot.

July 28, this morning died at Oldham Mary Newton, formerly of Bottom of Northmoor.

July 30th, this day at Hollinwood the quoiting match commenced betwixt John Cordwell, William Cordwell of Clifton and John Shaw of Greenacres moor, John Lawton of Waterhead Mill for 20 guineas each. 31 of up when the Cordwells being a great way ahead, Shaw and Lawton declined quoiting anymore and of consequence lost the wager.

August 6th, James Mills, formerly of Northmoor, attending a Carding Robin at Stockport, the leathern strap . . .

. . . caught him and taking him up, crushed him to death. Character: a civil, well-behaved peaceable man. Age 37 years.

August 6th, died the Earl of Guildford. He was Prime Minister during the American War. His age 60 years.

August 4th, died Lieutenant General Burgoyne.

August 3rd, died Sir Richard Arkwright, Knight.

August 11th, died Richard Booth, Formerly of Beartrees.

August 18th, the Assizes commenced at Lancaster when there was no Bill found against Mary Greathead. See her charge, page 11.

Sept.6th. This morning died Mary, wife of Philip Buckley of Busk. Disorder, a consumption.

September 14th, a son of John Bardsley's of Priest hill Oldham so much burnt that it died the next day aged 4 years.

September 22nd. This day John Turner of Oldham most shockingly bruised by a cow in Manchester that he was taken to the Infirmary with small hopes of recovery.

September 23rd, died in the greatest agonies William Winterbottom, who was so miserably wounded in May last (see page 18).

October 1st. This day at Newton Heath the quoiting match was decided in favour of the Cliftoners. For further particulars see page 24.

September 29th. James Walton, alias "Wrangle" committed to the New Bailey by Joseph Pickford Esq. charged with breaking the windows of John Whitehead of Maggot lane.

September 22nd, this day in Wheelers Manchester paper 228 innkeepers gave notice that they would not suffer any persons to have any seditious meetings in any of their respective houses. In Manchester alone number to be 228.

October 9th. Some very fine days last past but has been an uncommon wet summer, particularly the months of August and September.

September 28th. This day at Oldham, Richard Jackson of Bentbrow was married to one Betty Travis. There was something in the bride remarkable. She, a few days before, had swore a rape against James Cheetham of Oldham for which he was committed to prison, and about 5 weeks since she made oath that she was pregnant by one J. Ball, Ball was, of course, apprehended and gave bond to pay to the child. It now appears she is not with child.

Chadderton Hall, August 26th. Last night arrive Sir Watts and Lady Horton from London.

October 13th. This day at the conclusion of Manchester Sessions, James Walton was discharged, no Bill being preferred against him (see page 27) and John Sprewell of Littlemoor Lane found guilty of stealing Beers and Half Beers of cotton twist, the property of his late

Master, Mr. Joe Dunkerley, was imprisoned 21 days.

October 14th, this day died Hannah, wife of John Needham of Top o'th'Moor in the 89th year of her age. This venerable couple had been married 68 years and lived most of that time in a thatched cot where she died.

Page 30

Two wives in one house.

October 15th, this day, a severe conflict was fought at the house of James Fielding of Dolstile betwixt his real wife and a woman he had the audaciousness to marry. We hear Fielding and his sweet amourer decamped.

October 23rd, this day at the Prize Ringing at Rochdale, the first prize for Round Peals was given to the Ringers of Middleton. The Ringers of Oldham and Ashton disputing upon the condition of Change-Ringing, of course, there was no ringing for that prize.

Page 31

October 24th being the yearly Feast of Sick Club Societies of Oldham and its environs. The different members of clubs gave each, one halfpenny to the Rev. Mr. Wrigley and he preached them an excellent sermon in the Chapel from Romans 12th Chapter and 10th verse.

October 26th, damson plums sold at 6 pence per quart and other stone fruit in proportion. Bilberries sold last season 6 pence per quart and were exceeding scarce probably owing to the wetness of the last summer which was a very wet one. Apples sold at this time from 2 shillings to 2 shillings and sixpence per peck.

Page 32

October 27th, in the beginning of last month, one Jonathan Stansfield, on a courting party went to the house of Widow Howard of Hill-top where, he imprudently peeping through the window, received a wound which cut out one of his eyes and he, having the misfortune to lose one before, he is now in a state of darkness.

October 25th, this day at Failsworth, a quarrel arose bewixt Daniel Knot and James Tomlinson. Tomlinson kicked Knot over the bottom of his belly so fatally that he died on the l9th. The Coroner's Jury brought in manslaughter. Tomlinson, of course, was committed to Lancaster.

Page 33

Vice grown habitual then we find it is hard work to reclaim the mind. James Needham and Benjamin Butterworth charged with stealing ribbons in Oldham, were committed to the New Bailey, October 22nd. We sincerely wish that their misconduct may be a lesson to all unthinking youth of both sexes not to despise Reason and Justice nor sport with the laws of the land.

On Monday, November 5th, was observed as a day of public rejoicing and great bonfires in most part of places.

November 11th, this day at Oldham, one James Pearson, for being drunk during Divine Service, was by the Constables set in the Stocks. (*18)

Page 34

November 16th, owing to the uncommon wetness of the summer, potatos were exceeding scarce and dear and in some places the crops were so poor that the ground was never turned over for them. They were sold in general at 7s and 6d and 8s per load.

November l9th, a few days since was found at Rhodes, in a field of Mr. Joe Dunkerley's by a man who was working in the ground, the body of a new born child. The man cut it very much before he discovered it, and it was in a state of putrification. It must undoubtedly be the fruits of some vicious hand who hid it here to cover her shame.

December 3rd, uncommon fine weather, and has been for several weeks last past.

December 3rd, a great deal of commotion and strife in Great Britain in consequence of a certain pamphlet called Paine's "Rights of Man" (*19) so His Majesty was under the necessity of issuing out his proclamation against seditious writings.

December 7th, the people of Great Britain much divided and great commotions and strife concerning Paine's "Rights of Man".

Windsor, December 1st. This day His Majesty issued out his proclamation for the Parliament to meet on the 13th which was to have met on the 3rd January 1793, likewise for calling out part of the Militia and offering bountys to Seamen and Landsmen. This proclamation was in consequence of the tumults in several parts of England.

Samuel Taylor, Millwright of Oldham died December 12th.

Manchester, December 11th, there was a great meeting of the gentlemen of this town and neighbourhood, held this day at the Bulls Head, signing an address to His Majesty for his late proclamation, when the utmost confusion and riot ensued on the part of the Church and King. They broke the windows of Mr. Faulkner, printer of the Manchester Herald, and the windows of Mr. T. Walker. He fired a few shots amongst them which had the desired effect of dispersing them. It is said 3 were slightly wounded. The mob committed depradations most of the week and on the 12th they demolished the windows of a house in Newton Street. (*20)

In the latter end of this year the people most over England gave convincing proofs of their loyalty and in several places the effigy of Tom Paine was hanged, drawn and quartered etc. The month of December, the Navy and Army was recruited with the greatest Alacrity.

The End

1793

January 4th. This year commenced with very temperate weather for the Season, but people's minds far from temperate for a kind of frenzy has burst out amongst the people of this land under the cover of loyalty and shielded by the cries of Church and King, and King and Constitution have burst out of their disgust against the people that have countenanced the opinion of Thomas Paine. The effigy of Tom was burnt etc, in most towns and villages in England. In Oldham on New Year's Day his effigy was . . .

. . . with the greatest solemnity brought out of the dungeon and placed in a cart and from thence (attended by a Band of Music playing "God Save the King" besides sixty two musketeers) was taken to the gallow erected over a large Bonfire in the street where he was, for some time, hung by the neck and then let down to the fire and then consumed to ashes. (*21) A similar procession took place the same day in Failsworth and a very superb new pole was set up on the occasion and a large crown placed upon it.

Rushbearing at Failsworth Pole

January 6th, this morning was found near Newton Heath, James Lees of Greenacres Moor. He was returning from Manchester the night before and was starved to death.

January 8th, a few days since died Fanny Barns, butcher, Oldham.

January 8th, last night, Edmund Buckley of Busk for rude behaviour, lodged in the dungeon all night.

January 4th, this day was interred at Oldham, John Mellor of Stampstone, formerly an eminent singer.

January 9th, owing to the expectancy of an approaching war the lots for this part of the Lancashire Militia were this day drawn at Rochdale.

Manchester, January 3rd "The Strangers Friend Society", established here last winter, have again made the most minute researches into the miseries of human nature and have relieved a great number of objects and as usual made no enquiry of their Religion or Nation.

Betty, wife of Edmund Clegg of Burnley Lane died January 18th, disorder a fever, which all the family were attacked with at different periods - age 31 years.

January 22nd, an uncommon fine open winter thus far.

January 22nd, James Duckworth died at Chadderton Workhouse, aged 75 years.

Middleton, January 23rd, this day the New Militiamen for Manchester and Middleton Division were swore in at the Boars Head Inn here, and owing to the probability of a war substitutes were hired from 5 guineas and a half to 10 guineas.

January 26th at the conclusion of Manchester Sessions, James Needham and Benjamin Butterworth were discharged, no Bill being found. Their charge - see page 33 for 1792.

Uniform of the Lancashire Militia c. 1780

Manchester, January 26th, the recruiting business goes on with the greatest alacrity, in this place there being no fewer than 54 recruiting parties of different regiments.

James Rowland, Keeper of the Angel Inn, Oldham, died January 28th.

Alice, wife of James Woolstoncroft of Bottom of Northmoor died January 30th aged 75 years.

Oldham, January 29th. It is with extreme concern that we hear that on Saturday night last Nehemiah Ogden and John Lees went a courting to a young . . .

. . . woman who lived servant with George Scoles of Blackley. They all agreed to rob Mr. Scoles and the young woman fetched down a box which contained Bonds and notes to a considerable amount, besides upwards of 40 guineas in gold which they got clear off with. Suspicion falling on them, they were apprehended and all three committed to the New Bailey. We sympathise with their parents for they are persons of credit and respectability.

We hear that they were re-examined at the New Bailey on the 2nd February and on further proof were committed to the New Bailey.

Execution of Louis 16th King of France, January 21st. To enter into the merits or demerits would be too large a piece for such a small book. Suffice it is to say that he was born August 23rd 1754, crowned May 10th 1774, beheaded January 21st betwixt 10 and 11o'clock forenoon. News of the above arrived at London on the 25th January, at Manchester very early on the morning of the 27th January 1793.

February 5th it is as true as it is extraordinary that the French armies have a great deal of women in, who act both as officers and privates and at the late Battle at Hocheim two women in officer's uniforms were taken. One had received 3 wounds and the other that evening delivered of a fine boy.

George Wood of Bottom-of-Northmoor died February 8th age 65 years.

New burial ground Manchester February 10th Rev. Mr. Miles Wrigley performed the Burial Service when there were interred in one grave 11 coffins and 12 bodies, a woman and child being entombed in one coffin.

Preston, February 12th, this day the Royal Lancashire Militia were embodied here.

February 15th an excellent fine winter thus far.

Manchester, February 10th, it is as true as it is extraordinary that upwards of 1200 young men enlisted in the different Corps here in the course of the last 7 days as appeared in Harrops & Wheelers Manchester papers. (*22)

Thomas Townley Parker Esq. of Cureden, near Preston, High Sheriff for 1793.

Oldham February 6th, this day at the Angel Inn here there was a numerous and respectable meeting of the inhabitants of Oldham, Crompton, Chadderton and Royton. Joseph Pickford in the Chair: it was resolved to send an address to His Majesty which was signed by a great number of inhabitants.

January 12th, this day in Wheelers Manchester paper the landlords for the Division of Middleton testified their loyalty by signing an address dated December 22nd 1792. In Middleton 12, Royton 7, Crompton 9, Chadderton 7, Oldham 44 and the names of James Mills, Redtom Nook and James Clough of Lower Moor did not appear.

Ashton-under-Lyne 49, those at Rochdale appeared in a former paper.

February 1st, the French declare War against England and Holland.

February 11th, England declares War against France.

Manchester, February 19th, this day there was a meeting of the inhabitants here when they came to the resolution to assist Government when it was agreed to give 3 guineas extra advance to 500 Marines who should immediately enter in this town. A subscription was then entered into and £1200 was immediately subscribed.

Rochdale, February 25th this loyal town gives 4 Guineas over and above His Majesty's Bounty which makes 14 Guineas per man for a troop to be raised in this Parish for the 7th Regiment of Dragoons.

March 2nd, last night died Mary wife of James Woolstoncroft of Maggot-lane.

February 27th, in Jonathan Chadwicks of Wood 7 of that family which consisteth of 9 are at this time violently afflicted with a fever.

Sunday March 3rd, last night there was one of the most tremendous nights for wind ever remembered. It is impossible to describe its velocity or give a detail of the damages sustained here and in all the country south-west, for that was its direction. In this neighbourhood it drove down a deal of chimneys, blew down several barns and drove out several windows. At Manchester, it drove down 2 of the spires of the old Church, which made their way through the Church. One person was killed and a woman and child passing over the old wooden bridge, which railing was blown down have not since been heard of. The spires blown down had the Church and King's Colours fixed to them.

Oldham March 8th. Such is the rapid decrease of wages for fustian weaving and the universal pant for Glory that Thomas Dobson, James Cheltham and James Wolstoncroft of Northmoor entered into the Derbyshire Militia this day.

Middleton, March 12th, this day the Cheshire Militia on their route for Hull marched through here.

Northmoor, March 18th, this day the last of the Northmoor heroes marched off for Derby. Besides the 3 above mentioned in this page the following have enlisted into the Derbyshire Militia viz: Thomas Travis, James Hardy, Ned Hardy, Henry Newton . . .

Page 15

. . . Robert Heywood, James Bardsley, James Scofield, Mansfield, Newton, all of Northmoor.

Lancaster, March 11th, this day the inhabitants of Burnley-lane appeared at the court and Mr. Holt and his adherents submitted without trial which rids the Division of Streetbridge lane and a Fine of £480 and upwards which was infamously laid upon them. Council for the Poor Division, Mr. Law. Attorney, Mr. Josiah Phethian of Manchester.

Earl Barrymoor unfortunately shot near Dover, March 6th.

At Lancaster, March 11th, James Tomlinson, for killing Daniel Knot was imprisoned 8 months (see page 32 for 1792).

Page 16

Liverpool, March 20th, this day the Pelican Privateer of 18 gun and 120 men in going down the river suddenly sunk with all her people. About 20 were saved by boats putting out to their assistance.

War Office, March 8, an order was issued commanding all our pensioners to appear at different places in South Britain and Wales in conformity to the above one. Christopher Smith appeared at Manchester and was discharged in 1757 and was then 65 years old so that he consequently 101 years of age.

April 1st was Easter Monday was a very rough windy day attended with a great fall of snow.

March 4th this day William Lawson entered on the Angel Inn, Oldham.

Page 17

Heywood, March 27 this day Captain Starkey of Redivalls near Bury beat up here and listed 13 young men when his relation Mr. Starkey of this place gave each recruit 2 Guineas and roasted 2 sheep and gave plenty of ale. E. G. Haywood likewise gave each recruit 1 Guinea.

April 5th, this day at Oldham the Manchester Marine Corps came - attended by a few landlords and a band of music and two elegant flags or Colours. On the recruiting business the Rev. John Griffith attended to a test those that were enlisted. Some four Oldham men did enter in.

Page 18

Manchester, April 10th, this morning one Sergeant Shaw of Ashton-under-Lyne cut his throat in so shocking a manner that he died soon after.

April 14th died Susan, wife of Robert Lees of Top o'th'moor.

Monday April 15th, this day a most tremendous cold windy day attended with a great fall of snow.

About the beginning of this year the people of this land tasted once more of adversity by a general failure in business.

Manchester April 19th being the Sessions here Lees & Ogden were discharged, no Bill being found for their Charge. See page 6 and 7.

Page 19

April 21st it is with heartfelt concern that everyday furnishes us with accounts from all parts of the Country of the distressed situation of the poor.

April 19th. A general fast throughout England and Wales.

Oldham April 23, this morning died the Reverend Hugh Grimshaw, Minister of this place.

April 25th, this morning died Eley Duckworth of Burnley lane, disorder a fever, age 28 years.

April 26th, died Anne, wife of William Whittaker of Top o' th'Moor. Disorder Childbed.

Oldham, April 27th, this day died Abraham Beswick, formerly Schoolmaster.

Manchester, April 29th last week Messrs Jones, Barker & Lloyd stopped payments at their Bank here.

Manchester April 27th this day in the Potato Market 120 loads which were short of weight were seized for the use of the poor. May 7th, the most unexampled misery is supported by the poor people, owing to the failure of allsorts of business. Great numbers of people are without work.

Manchester May 6th. This day a dispute arose betwixt the officers of the Yorkshire Militia and the populace which terminated in very serious circumstances.

Manchester May 11th. This day potatos sold 11 shillings per load.

May 12th. Every day and every hour furnishes us with fresh instances of the times. Money is not to be obtained on any account whatever so that the poor are in the most wretched situation imaginable.

May 29th. It has been uncommon fine weather for one month past. There has scarcely been a drop of rain 'til this day when it rained a little and then terminated in a severe shower of snow.

June 1st. For several nights past very severe frosts in so much that it has destroyed a deal of blossoms and buds.

"You that have feelings for a tear
Give nature vent and drop it here".

The poor of this neighbourhood and country in general, at this time experience the most torturing misery owing to the dearness of every necessary of life and the scarceness of work and the uncommon low wages.

June 11th. In the months of May and June subscriptions were set on foot in Manchester, Oldham, Hollinwood etc and relief thereby given to the starving poor.

June 14th, Abraham Crossley, Chandler of Royley died. Disorder a rupture.

Manchester June 15. There is a great bustle here at present owing to some of the Constitutional Society being taken up whereof some are committed to the New Bailey and some to Lancaster, but more of this in some future page.

June 15th at Oldham this day New Potatos sold at 4 pence per pound and gooseberries at 8 pence per Quart.

Oldham, June 22nd, potatoes 3½ pence per pound and gooseberries 5 pence per Quart.

Manchester June 22nd. Old potatos sold at 11s 6d per load.

Oldham, June 26th. This day Sergeant Clough arrived wanting a few recruits for the Derbyshire Militia. Such was the pant in the path of Glory that a great number of recruits flocked to his Standard so that his order was soon stacked and it is supposed he might have had hundreds more, had he wanted them.

Oldham July 4th. New potatos 3 and a half pence per pound. Of an inferior sort 5 farthings per pound.

Manchester, June 29th. Old potatos sold at 10 and 6d to 13 shillings per load.

Oldham, July 5th. This morning died William Frith, Stationer and Book Binder.

Josuah Horton Esquire of Holroyd, Yorkshire, interred at Oldham, July 6th.

Busk, July 8th. This day a swarm of bees from place unknown hived in an old pigeon box of Tom Cheethams here, and they supposing them to be of a dangerous tendency, got scalding water and destroyed them.

Thursday July 18th. Some fine rain fell which with some cool breezes made it more pleasant than it has been for some time for on the 11th it was so excessive hot that it was supposed to be the hottest day ever felt in this country and in the South of England, several men whilst labouring in the fields dropped down dead.

Page 26

Manchester, Saturday July 27th. This day at the Sessions here, Benjamin Booth, for uttering treasonable expressions was found guilty. Sentence 12 months imprisonment.

Royton, July 31st. This day at the Sessions here, Susan Mills, upon complaint of the Overseer of Chadderton, for having born a bastard child, committed to the New Bailey for one year.

August 3rd, this day the remains of Joseph, son of James Andrew of Boggardhole were interred and while the funeral rites were performing, his brother John expired. Disorder, a spotted or putrid fever (*23). Ages, John 20, Joseph 18 years of age.

Page 27

August 3rd. Most tremendous cracks of thunder with vivid flashes of lightning with very heavy showers of rain. This day the lightning set a hedge of fire near Chadderton.

August 11th. The relentless cruelty exercised by the Fustian Masters upon the poor weavers is such that it is exampled in the annals of cruelty, tyranny and oppression for it is nearly an impossibility for weavers to earn the common necessities of life so that a great deal of families are in the most wretched and pitiable situation.

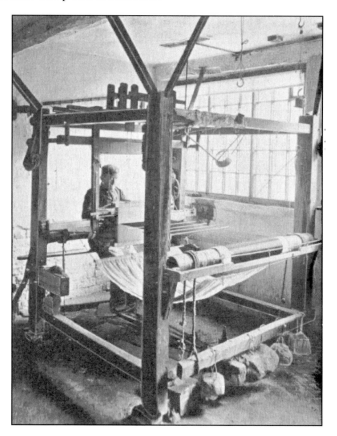

Handloom Weaving

Oldham, August 17th. This day, one Sarah Fielding and her son, a boy of 11 years of age of Shaw were detected stealing shoes in Oldham for which the woman was committed and the boy discharged.

Oldham Rushcart

Page 28

Saturday, August 31st, this day being Oldham Rushbearing, owing to the adversity of the times was very thinly attended and graced only with 3 rush carts, that is one from Cowhill, one from Hollins, one from Greenacres Moor (and)

On Sunday September 1st was an uncommon wet day so that very few strangers attended the Wakes at Oldham. It was observable at these Wakes that people having but little money in their pockets were consequently better behaved than at any former Wakes.

In Wheelers Manchester Chronicle of August 31st, it appeared that since January last, owing to these dismal times, no less than 873 Commissions of Bankruptcy had been issued out.

Page 29

Thursday, September 5th. A very large eclipse of the sun. There had not been one so large since one on the sun in April 1764.

September 8th. The remains of John Smith of Dolstile were interred at Oldham this day. He was one of the oldest Fustian Manufacturers in the Parish of Oldham and died poor.

Chadderton Hall, September 9th. This day the archers commenced the shooting in the park here, when the quiver of 4 pairs of arrows, the gift of Lady Horton was won by Mr. Hobson.

September 24th. Meal sold in this neighbourhood at 22d per peck, which a fortnight since sold at 2s 2d per peck.

October 6th. It rose to 1s 11d per peck.

Page 30

Blocklane, October 5th. Last night the house of Henry Whittaker of this place was broke open and robbed of various articles. On the 8th they apprehended Joseph Hilton and searched his house when several articles were owned which had been stolen, and on the 9th Hilton was committed to the New Bailey.

October 10th, this day Robert Sutcliffe of Huntlane died at an advanced age.

October 12th, uncommon fine weather and has been so for some time so that swarms of gnats attend the evenings as in summer and bats are constantly seen at night.

Page 31

October 15th, last night some villains cut down a pear tree of James Clegg's of Northmoor. Likewise the hen roost of Ashton Ogden of Northmoor robbed of a hen the same night.

October 16th. Yesterday at Manchester the trade fell much lower than it had been for some time so that it is impossible for the poor to subsist much longer, for provisions are excessively dear.

Meal 2s per peck; Flour 2s to 2s 2d per peck; Cheese 4d to 5d per pound; butter old 8½d per pound; New 10d per pound; Sugar 7d and 9d per pound; treacle 3½d per pound; Beef 4½ per pound; Mutton 5d per pound. Potatos at Manchester 5s Per load: at home 10d per strike. Malt 1s 9d per pound.

Page 32

October 16th. This day being Oldham Fair, owing to the fineness of the weather was numerously attended but owing to the scarceness of money very little business was done except in the Military line for there never was so many recruiting sergeants at any one time here, before there was a few young men enlisted.

Oldham October 16th, this day Mr. Jacob Radcliff of Bank here, generously gave a fat cow to be divided amongst the most necessitous poor. This is the second generous act of this worthy gentleman.

Page 33

Manchester, Saturday October 19th, at the Sessions here, Joseph Hilton for breaking the houses of Henry Whittaker and Standerings in the fields was for the last offence transported for 7 years (see page 30).

There was a Bill against Sarah Fielding (see page 27). She was bailed out of the New Bailey when she had been in about a fortnight. Sentence 8 months imprisonment New Bailey.

Oldham October 23rd. This day the Sick Club Societies attended Divine Service when the Rev. Mr. Wrigley preached at the chapel. His text Romans 12th Chapter, verses 4th and 5th.

Sarah Fielding died the day before the term of her imprisonment was out in the New Bailey.

Page 34

It is worthy of remark that in the Sick Club at Samuel Horrocks, Oldham since the Feast Day 1792 to the Feast Day 1793 upwards of forty members have enlisted and marched in the different regiments.

The celibrated Lord George Gordon died prisoner in Newgate London October 31st.

Execution of Maria Antoinetta, late Queen of France, at Paris October 16th. She was born November 2nd 1755.

Oldham, Nov 6th. On Monday the 4th at night the house of James Potter of Boggardhole was broke open and this day Joseph Needham was committed to the New Bailey to take his trial for the same.

Page 35

November 17th. Sir Watts Horton, Birthday aged 40 years.

Mary, daughter of Edmund Mellor of Top o'th'Moor died November 22nd age 21 years.

Ann, wife of Jonathan Woolstoncroft died November 25th. Bottom of Maygate lane.

November 29th. Excellent fine weather and has been so for some time.

November 29th, this day Sir Watts and Lady Horton, with a grand retinue, left Chadderton Hall for London.

December 8th uncommon fine thus far having been neither a gleam of frost or snow.

Page 36

December 8th. We find that the price of labour daily decreases. The Hatters have dropped one half of their wages. Callicoes are wove for 3 shillings per cut. 26 check at 7 shillings per piece. In the Fustian Branch their misery is inconceivable. Velveretts being worked with 18 or 19 lb of weft in, for 18 shillings and so in proportion which caused a great deal of Heads of family to enlist in this country (*24).

December 13th. This morning James Rowbottom died aged 16 years. He had been sick for upwards of 5 years which . . .

. . . sickness he bore with the greatest patience and Christian fortitude which was never much surpassed of any person of riper years.

December 19. Last evening was attended with loud cracks of thunder and vivid flashes of lightning.

December 23rd. Butchers meat at this time is thought reasonable. The very best of beef is sold at 4 pence per pound. Inferior pieces at 3 pence per pound, Mutton at 4 pence halfpenny, some at 4 pence per pound; onions at $3^1/_2$ pence per pound, apples from 16 pence to 20 pence per peck; Treacle $4^1/_2$ pence per pound.

December 29th. The fine weather, which has been so fine as never was known terminated in a very keen frost last night.

Fine Winter, December 28, to this time the weather has been so open and fine as much to resemble Spring. The air continually warm and all sorts of vegetation approaching very fast. Pollianthus, primroses, Whiterocks, Spice, Gilliflower etc in full bloom.

December 31st, the year concludes with a cold boistrous day and the calamitys and miserys of the poor too heavy to bear, and when it will end human wisdom cannot tell.

Manchester, December 28th. This day Meal dropped a few shillings per load as it did on the 21st.

The Recruiting business goes on with the greatest alacrity. The 12th Regiment of foot, the 33rd (*25) of foot have picked up a great deal of both young men and a great deal of middle-aged married men in Oldham and its environs. The year 1793 is now concluded and I hope for more happiness and less misery the next year.

FINIS

1794

January 1st. This year commenced on Wednesday which was an uncommon fine day but owing to the failure of all sorts of businesses there was very little Christmas cheer, for very few families were able to buy Malt and brew. Roast beef and pies were not to be seen, so that the poor, after a years misery meet with a wretched Christmas treat, for as the old year concluded with unparalleled misery, the New Year does not commence with better appearances but may the Almightly God of . . .

. . . His Great goodness grant that things may have a happier turn that the poor may have their bellys full which are now very much short.

1 day Joseph Scholes having got a recruiting order for the 57th Regiment of foot, beat up in Oldham in a superb new suit of clothes.

> "Tis easy into Hell to fall
>> But to get out again is all"

We are very sorry to say that on the 2nd Joseph Garlick was committed to Lancaster charged with stealing a mare, the property of Mr. H. Lees of Ashton-under-Lyne.

3rd. Joseph Lee of Chadderton and 2 of his sons were apprehended for stealing fish off Sir Watts Horton when Joseph was commited to Lancaster and his two sons suffered to enlist.

8th. Abraham Ogden of Nathanroe interred at Oldham.

8th. 47 recruits of the 80th Regiment marched up Burnley Lane in their route from Bolton to Doncaster.

9th. John Ogden of Cockhouse, Oldham interred this day.

9th. Martha Taylor of Scolesfold interred this day.

13th. An uncommon fine thawing day.

13th. Being the Newmarket at Rochdale there was a great deal of Sergeants beat up and offered large bountys for recruits.

15th. Wife of Thomas Jackson of Priesthill, Oldham died in childbed of the 16th. Child was interred at the Methodist Chapel and being the first body buried there caused a great concourse of people.

22nd. As a proof of the influence which the Military have over the fair sex a young woman possessed with less virtue . . .

. . . than beauty, decamped from the 'Cotton Tree' Oldham with one of the train of Artillery, but by the timely interference of her friends this affair was quashed in its infancy.

23rd. The young woman and the soldier who decamped from the 'Cotton Tree' Tavern were privately married at Stockport.

22nd. Captain Blairs of the 12th of foot with his Sergeant Hammond with a large retinue of recruits beat up in a very sumptuous style this day at Oldham.

22nd. This day Wednesday the Sessions commenced at the New Bailey Manchester when Joseph Needham, for stealing a powder horn at the house of James Potter, Boggardhole, Oldham. Sentence 6 months imprisonment and privately whipped (see page 34 for 1793).

25th. This day an uncommon cold day attended with a very high wind and snow. At night it terminated in freezing.

John Clegg

Hannah Clegg (nee Dawson), John Clegg's wife

Bent Hall, Oldham

27th. Captain Horsfall of 39th of foot roasted a sheep and gave it with bread and potatos to the populace in Oldham, where his Sergeant and Sergeant Hammond, 12th of foot, Sergeant Hollinworth, of 33rd of foot, beat up in a very superb style.

Page 7

January 1794. 25th. The miserys of the poor it seems are not up to the utmost height of wretchedness for at Manchester this day Mr. Hibbert dropped his Velveretts to 18 shillings per piece.

31st. Last night the weather turned to a very rapid thaw.

31st. Mr. John Clegg of Bent Hall, Oldham, Hat Manufacturer died in an advanced age.

31st. Mr. Robert Taylor of Mumps died. The different vicissitude of fortune experienced by this man ought to be a useful lesson to Mankind. In the early part of his time he fully experienced misery and in a little time he arrived at the utmost pitch of splendour, but at his death his affairs were in a deranged situation.

Page 8

February 1794. 1st day. Landlord of the York Minster Tavern, Manchester, hanged himself this morning. Likewise a woman hanged herself on the 29th in Manchester.

6th. The recruits of the 12th Regiment of foot marched from Oldham on their route for Drogedea in Ireland. The concourse of people that witnessed their heroic departure was immense. They showed a deal of martial spirit and took leave of their friends who wished them luck, with a deal of manly fortitude they were led up by a drum and Etches the fiddler.

Page 9

February 1794. When the drum ceased which was at the Methodist Chapel, Etches struck up the old tune of (I lost my love and I care not, I can have another I fear not). The whole number consisted of 36, all from Oldham and its environs. The following is a list of a part of them, viz John Hide, Samuel Duredin, John Taylor, Robert Buckley, James Hall of Oldham, Sawney Radcliffe, James Whitehead of Coulthurst lane, Robert Law of Edge lane, John Needham, Jonas Scofield, James Scofield of Maggot-lane, Joseph Scott, John Taylor, John Ogden, Ben Needham of Northmoor, John Whitehead of Burnley Brow, Thanial Stott, Joseph Mellor, John Duckworth, John Bennet of Cowhill . . .

Page 10

. . . Josuah Taylor of Cotthurst Highbarn, who were all married men and most of them large families. John Ogden, Abraham Cheetham, John Ogden of Northmoor, James Whitehead of Coulthurst lane, single men some few were turned again to stay a recruiting. The following had gone at a former time in the said Regiment viz: John Kay of Busk, Abraham Crompton, James Taylor, Thomas Pattin, James Marlor of Oldham, George Wolstoncroft of Maggot-lane, John Etches of Failsworth, James Newton, John Newton of Oldham. Single men marched on the 6th but were not mentioned in their proper place. Their bounties were from 10 to 12 Guineas each.

Page 11

February 1794. Henry Philip Houghton Esquire of Houghton, High Sheriff 1794, he his son of Sir Henry Houghton Bart.

8th. Hannah, wife of James Chadwick of Old clarks having experienced the greatest miserys and want died in the greatest agonies.

9th. At Manchester Sessions which concluded January 25th, eleven persons received sentence of transportation for 7 years each.

5th. There was a meeting at Oldham Workhouse to take into consideration the oppressive actions of the Rev.Thomas Fawcett concerning the Church fees.

Page 12

February 1794. 10th. Onions sold at Oldham. Three pence per pound.

15th. At Manchester this day the wages at Check Weaving were dropped 1 shilling per piece and fustian warps 44 yards, sold 4 pence per Beer.

16th. Sunday a mad dog made its appearance in Oldham - did considerable damage and threw the inhabitants into the the greatest consternation.

18th. An uncommon fine day. Much appearance of Spring this morning, was welcomed in by the melodious songs of the Thrush, Sparrow, Goldfinch, Red Robin and Flaxfinch with the lark.

19th. Old Isaac Whittaker Taylor of Oldham and Jane, wife of William Haywood of Bent Oldham both interred this day.

20th. As a proof of the forwardness of the Spring there is at this time a Pilewort in full bloom.

15th. Mutton raised to 5 pence per pound at Oldham this day.

22nd. John Buckley, Busk, entered (as) a private in the Oxford Blues.

27th. An uncommon fine Spring thus far.

28th. A general fast observed through England and Wales.

March 1794.

2nd. Manchester, potatos sold 6 shillings per load here this day.

On the 27th of last month Henry Smethurst of Oldham was interred at Oldham.

6th (word obliterated) did appear to tyrannise and domineer.

8th. An account of the forwardness of the Spring a robin's nest was found.

8th. A party of recruits of the 33rd Regt of foot, consisting of 16, marched from Oldham on their route for Dublin (their order was postponed, they came back to Oldham same day).

March 1794.

9th. It appears that 20 men in Oldham have enlisted within these few weeks who have left 20 wives and 79 children, as appeared in the Chester paper of the 7th instant.

10th. The recruits of the 57th Regiment of foot raised in Oldham by Sergeant Scholes marched off on their route to the Isle of Wight. They consisted of about 20 of whom were James Needham, Joseph Needham of Maggot lane, Ben Bardsley, Tom Chadderton etc. etc., both of Oldham. On the same day an order arrived for the remainder of the 12th Regiment of foot to march to join their respective corps.

March 1794. 15th. A sergeant belonging to the 33rd of foot quartered at Robert Smethursts, Oldham, was attached with a fit and immediately expired.

12th. In consequence of these dreadful times, it is a fact that Jonathan Cheetham, overseer of the poor of Oldham, relieved upwards of 160 families, exclusive of those in the workhouse on this day.

15th. Veal sold 6 pence per pound at Ben Ward's, Oldham.

19th. John Needham of Top o'th'Moor died very suddenly age 91 years.

March 1794 18th. The recruits of the 33rd Regiment of foot marched out of Oldham on their route for Dublin.

21st. The weather which has been wet and cold for the last 12 days turned to a very fine Spring day.

22nd. James Scofield, late of Scolesfold, Maggot lane, private in the 12th of foot interred at Liverpool this day. The cause of his death, a fever.

24th. The recruiting business still goes on briskly. At Oldham Sergeants Scoles and Hammond with a sergeant of Col. Hewets beat up this day.

April 1794. 1st day. Last week Abraham Jackson, commonly called Strandring John Scofield, both of Northmoor, and Samuel Ogden of Oldham enlisted into the 99th of foot.

1st day. Last week at Middleton 20 men enlisted into the different Corps, there 18 of whom were swore in.

6th. One James Mayal of Lees dropped down dead while attending Divine Service in Oldham Chapel.

7th. Jonathan Cheetham, overseer of Oldham relieved upwards of seventy wives whose husbands are at this time soldiers.

April 1794. 12th. George Rowbottom listed into M. E. Balfour's Regiment of foot.

12th Colonel Beaumont Light horse consisting of 50 men marched through Oldham on their way to Beverly.

13th. Robert Ogden Boxmaker, Oldham died.

On the 31st of March the Assizes opened at Lancaster when Joseph Lee was acquitted. See page 3 for 1794.

. . . and Joseph Garlick was sentenced to 7 years transported. See his charge, page 2, 1794.

April 1794. Likewise at the above Assizes the trial of Mr. Walker and others charged with seditious practices. He was honorably acquitted. Dunn, the evidence against them, was committed for perjury.

18th. This week Thomas Shalcross, Blacksmith, Oldham, Robert Crompton, James Newton of Top 'o'th'Moor enlisted into the Yorkshire Rangers.

20th. James Buckley sworn into M. E. Balfour's Regiment of foot.

21st. Being Easter Monday a match of football (*26) was played at Northmoor betwixt the batchelors and married, which was won by the latter.

April 1794. 21st. Royton Mob.

In consequence of an advertisement for a meeting to address his Majesty for a reform in Parliament, the gentlemen who met for the above purpose were inhumanly treated by a merciless mob (*27).

21st. A large meeting of the Weavers on Newton Heath in order to advance the price of wages.

28th. The recruiting business goes on with the greatest alacrity in all parts of the country.

May 1794. 2nd. This was Oldham fair and being a very fine day was uncommonly crowded. There was a great deal of recruiting sergeants which made a very fine show, particularly a party of the Hon. William Ashton Harbord's lighthorse from Middleton.

6th. A party of the Manchester volunteers with a fine band of music passed through Burnley lane on their way to Oldham.

10th. New potatos sold at Manchester. Ten pence per pound.

On the 24th of April upwards of 20 recruits raised in Middleton for Lord Fielding's Lighthorse marched for Coventry.

May 1794. 14th. This morning died Ester, wife of Edward Duckworth of Denton Lane. Disorder childbed age 41 years and on the same day was interred at Oldham the remains of John Shallcross of the Coldstream Regiment of footguards. His funeral was attended with all the military pomp imaginable.

16th. This day gooseberries sold in Manchester market 2 pence per quart.

On the 2nd of this month at Oldham fair, Michael Rowbottom had his pocket picked of his pocket book containing two Bills of Exchange but had the happiness to get one again on it being offered at Chester.

May 1794. A Real Fact.

On the 25th of January last, during that severe wind for which see page 6, the gibbit and body of William Henry Clarke, hung near Northwich for robbing the mail, was blown down and the body has not since been heard of.

24th. It is with the greatest satisfaction that we hear that the price of labour in this country is considerably advancing.

26th. Edmund Buckly of Busk died, age 35 years. Disorder fits which he had been afflicted with a long time.

May 1794. 26th. Mr. Hollinworth attended by a large number of Freemasons.

Two elegant flags and a band of music beat up for Colonel Hewitts Regiment of Foot in Oldham and its environs.

26th. Lord Shuffield's regiment of Light Horse marched from Middleton on their route for Norfolk.

29th. This day was ushered in with ringing of bells, decorating their doors with oak boughs etc. etc. and such was the call for oak in Manchester that boughs sold from 3 pence to 1 shilling to 1s and 6 pence a piece (*28).

June 1794. 13th. Died Jane wife of Thomas Mills of Red Tom Nook in a very advanced age.

16th. A general illumination through Oldham on the glorious victory obtained by Lord Howe (*29).

18th. New potatos sold at Oldham, five farthings per pound.

21st. Uncommon hot and large honey falls for several days last past.

25th. New potatos sold at Oldham, one pound per penny; an inferior sort one pound and half per penny.

June 1794. 26th. Uncommon fine weather and has been for some time past.

30th Last night a very large honey fall.

July 1794. 8th. Josuah Woolstoncroft, Hatter of Oldham, died at an early age. Disorder, consumption.

13th. Robert Marlor of Top o'th'Moor, an eminent country fiddler died. Disorder, a consumption.

14th. The remains of Daniel Broadbent, commonly called 'Dan of Burns' late of Hollinwood but last of Bengall Street Manchester were interred.

July 1794. 15th. Was interred at Oldham the remains of Old John Winterbottom, late of Lees Hall and a son of Charles Stotts of Royton which had been missing since the day before was found dead in a sandhole near Royton. His age 6 years.

17th. One Cheetham aged 22 years was drowned whilst bathing near Pawden.

19th. The Bishop of Chester passed down Burnley Lane on his way to Middleton, where the day following he confirmed 300 children.

July 1794. 22nd. The Bishop of Chester confirmed 4461 children at Manchester this day.

31st. It is worthy of observation that this summer has been a very fine one, but rather too dry this month. Has been excessive hot, attended with great honey falls.

On the 21st it begun to rain moderately 'til this and still continues to rain which will greatly increase vegetation.

23rd. The Sessions commenced at Manchester and concluded on the 29th when Smith; Thorp; Berry and Seddon were convicted of assaulting Whittaker in Failsworth on the 22nd of April last on the pretence of his being a Jacobin . . .

July 1794. . . . when two of them were sentenced to Lancaster for 6 months. Each one in the said Jail for 3 months, one in the New Bailey for 2 months and Knight of Saddleworth, a noted Jacobin, for wounding in his own defence one Joseph Taylor at Royton on the 21st April last, sentenced to 2 years imprisonment at Lancaster; and John Taylor of Royton for defending one of his neighbours from the cruelties of the mob at Royton on the 21st April, one months imprisonment at the New Bailey . . .

July 1794. . . . and John Buckley and James Wood for assaulting the House of James Clegg of Northmoor, 14 days imprisonment in the New Bailey.

30th. There were the greatest number of gooseberries this year ever remembered. They sold from one penny to three pence per Quart; bilberries, notwithstanding there was a great number sold 4 pence per Quart.

31st. John Bardsley, commonly called John Titus died at Boggard hole Oldham.

August 1794. 1st. 'The turbulent spirit of the wicked gave proof of its vice'.

3rd. It is with heartfelt pleasure that we hear Calicoes, Nankeens, Roe Moll, Napkins and all sorts of light goods are at this time rapidly rising their wages. Likewise, hats are increasing prodigiously, but poor strong Fustian remains in its former miserable situation.

16th. It is with pleasure that I announce that the wages of Nankeens rose this day 3 shillings per piece and jeand nankeens 4 shillings per piece.

August 1794. 16th. In Wheelers Manchester paper of this day a reward of 10 Guineas is offered for the apprehending of Joseph Garlick, who it appears made his escape on Finchly Common as they were convening him in order to be transported. He escaped on the 6th of August.

23rd. Manchester this day the wages of Gimmams (ginghams) was raised to 24 shillings and 4 pence per end. In December last it was wove at 16 shillings per end. In April last 19 shillings.

August 1794. 23rd. Being Middleton Rushbearing Saturday it was very throng and there were 9 carts and one wagon.

30th. Was Oldham Rushbearing Saturday. Owing to the poorness of the times there was only 3 rushcarts, one from Northmoor, one from Cowhill, one from Greenacres. They were all fully decked with emblems of Royalty. Oldham was very thinly attended except soldiers who made deal of manoeuvres to gain recruits and gave from 10 to 15 Guineas for recruits.

September 1794. 10th. Lady Horton gave an elegant quiver of arrows which were shot for in the park at Chadderton Hall and won by Mr. Thackery and the same day Thomas, son of James Tetlow was killed by the kick of a horse. He was imprudently plucking hairs out of his tail at Dolstile.

14th. The astonishing demands for all sorts of light goods surpasses belief. The wages of Dimities, Gingams, Nankeens. Checks is rapidly advancing.

September 1794. The follow is the order which was given out last Quarter Sessions at Manchester concerning Streetbridge Lane.

Sir Watts Horton begins at the guide post in Chadderton lane and takes .	126 yards
Burnley Lane Division	200
Royle & Sir Watts Horton	283
Burnley Lane division	81
Adam Whitworth	53
Sir W. Horton.	94
James Holt	16

27th. Last night died . . . wife of Samuel Fletcher, innkeeper, bottom of Greenacres Moor. A son aged 21 years was buried this week. Their disorders, a fever.

September 1794. 18th. George Rowbottom of the 93rd of foot arrived from Londonderry.

26th. Last night Michael Rowbottom was thrown from his horse and very much bruised.

29th. Monday, Peter Whitehead formerly an eminent singer died very suddenly in Oldham Workhouse, age 74 years. He was taken to have been buried on Wednesday but the upright priest would not bury him and he was left on a tombstone all night and was buried on Thursday, the day following.

October 1794. 4th. Betty, wife of Jonathan Raynor, Innkeeper Oldham, drowned herself at Hollinwood.

2nd. The Rochdale Volunteers commanded by John Entwhistle Esquire arrived at Royton and fired several volleys. Mr. Pickford treated them with a roasted sheep and plenty of porter.

11th. John Grime, a man famous in the flower gardens died near Royton after a long illness.

12th Betty, wife of Mr. Thomas Whittaker, Oldham died in Childbed.

October 1794. 22nd. Being the Sick Club Feast in Oldham, upwards of 1200 members from the different societys assembled when Mr. Pearcey preached in the Chapel from Corinthians 1st Chapter 16, verse 2.

17th At the Sessions at Manchester, Robert Baxter for stealing woollen cloth transported for 7 years.

25th At Manchester this day, they beat up for the Lancashire Fencebles (*30) for the first time.

November 1794. 5th . A Bull Bait in Oldham and the Lancashire Fencebles head by Captain Wm. Horton beat up in great style (*31).

15th James Buckly with about 100 recruits for the 93rd marched off for Londonderry.

19th John Ogden, Jenny maker of Fog lane died. Disorder, a consumption.

29th Peggy, wife of Titus Bardsley of Maggot lane died. Disorder a consumption.

1st. Yesterday, Robert Gregg Hopwood of Hopwood attained the age of 21 years when there was ringing of bells and other demonstrations of joy in all the neighbouring towns.

14th Uncommon wet weather and no appearance of frost so that it has been unfavourable to the getting up of potatos which have sold from 5 to 6 shillings per load and consequently the farmer has not been able to get in his wheat which, it is feared, will advance the price of that article.

December 1794. 21st. John Shallcross of Oldham, formerly an emminent Blacksmith died in advanced age. And Grace, wife of Abraham Colling of Chadderton died at the great age of 80 years.

14th. Robert Radcliffe Esquire of Foxdenton Birthday age 21 years. Ringing on the occasion at Middleton and Oldham.

24th. The Lancashire Volunteers fenceble being upwards of 1000 men were reviewed at Manchester by Major General Scott and all returned fit for duty.

December 1794.

31st. The year 1794 is now nearly concluded and all things have a dreary appearance for nothwithstanding there is the greatest demand for Nankeens, and other light goods, owing to the low wages given and the dearness of all the necessaries of life it is impossible for persons with large familys to get what nature requires. The Minister has again set up the war whoop which is a harbinger for future miserys for by the sound of the martial drum and the alluring sergeant . . .

Page 45

. . . holding in his hand a bounty of from ten to twenty five Guineas per man, and pressed on all sides by the greatest necessity causes a great deal of husbands to leave their virtuous wives and darling children. "May God at his great goodness take us poor under his protection and preserve us from such pressing necessities and wants" is the order prayer and sincere wish of (unreadable).

The End

1795

January 1795. 1st. This year commenced on Thursday, which was a very fine day but owing to the poverty of most of the familys the ancient hospitality was nearly forgotten. Roast beef and pies were more scarce than last Christmas so that misery dwells on every countenance and there is the greatest reason to be apprehensive of the sorrows which are hovering round.

2nd. Jacob Radcliffe, ever famed for his benevolence, killed a cow and gave it to the poor.

January 1795. 17th. James Mellor, a person famed for simpleness and peacebleness died at Chadderton Workhouse.

21st. Hannah, wife of George Wood of Winnock, died, disorder a consumption. Age 33 years.

Friday 16th, Saturday 17th, Monday 19th. The Lancashire Volunteers marched through Middleton on their route to Doncaster, Pontefract, Rotherham, Wakefield and Bawtry. They were as usual attended by a large group of females.

January 1795. 26th. A child so shockingly burned near Chadderton Workhouse that it died the next day.

27th. An uncommon thawing day. The waters rose uncommonly high.

28th. A rough, snowy, windy day.

31st. For several days last past, uncommon cold frosty weather and the wages of light goods decreasing and all the necessaries of life rapidly increasing.

February 1795. 2nd. One petitions for peace with France and the other to carry on the war with spirit were signed by the different parties at Oldham (*32).

4th. Oldham, a large quantity of coals were given to the most necessitous poor this day.

11th. Oldham, loaves were distributed to the poor of Oldham this day.

14th. Nankeens dropped 2 shillings a piece this day.

16th. Great subscriptions for relief of the poor in most parts of England.

February 1795. Robinson Shuttleworth, High Sheriff this year. Lives at Preston.

17th. Every necessary of life rises astonishingly so that the poor are in a most lamentable condition.

18th. A bitter cold day and a very strong frost.

24th. The storm still continues with unabating fury.

25th. A general fast kept throughout England etc.

March 1795. 4th. It began to thaw very finely this morning.

5th. A very fine thawing day so that the frost which commenced on the 22nd December last, in all probability will dissolve.

12th. Died Josuah Kershaw of Top o th' Moor, aged 74 years.

18th. On the 14th, it commenced a severe frost and snow on this day, it terminated in a thaw.

March 1795. 20th. Joseph Newton was interred at Oldham. He died far advanced in years. Was a pensioner and once served in the East Indies and the same day a letter was received from Plymouth giving an account of the death of James Cowper, formerly of Cowhill. Taylor and Matthew Barnes, formerly of Oldham, shoemaker, both in the 91st Regiment.

21st. Thomas Butterworth, late of Fog Lane, wheelwright, died in the West Indies in the 13th Regiment of Foot. Received that account this day.

March 1795. 22nd. It is with heartfelt concern that we hear of the lowering of wages for weaving Nankeens are dropped 5 shillings per piece, dimitis 8s per piece and most kind of weaving in proportion.

14th. The Assizes commenced at Lancaster, when Messrs. Shallcross, Pearson and Knight appearing to a Bill of Indictment for rioting at Royton, April 21st 1794. Judge Heath, on hearing 4 of the Plaintiffs witnesses who were Church and King, give such a scandalous account . . .

. . . of their treatment towards the defendents that he would not suffer any more witnesses to be examined, but honourably acquitted the defendants. Council for the defendants, Messrs. Vaughan, Chamber, Lloyd and Heywood and Cockell for Plaintiffs Messrs. Law, Topping, Wood and Johnson.

27th. Last night died Joseph Wilde, Bottom of Couldhurst Lane in the 65th year of his age.

March 1795. 28th. As a proof of the distress which the poor suffer at this time the following is a true statement of the different necessities of life, viz:

Meal	1s 11d	per peck
Flour	2s 4d	per peck
an inferior sort	2s 2d	per peck
Malt	1s 10d	per peck
Potatos	10d	per stroke
Treacle	4d	per pound
New butter	10d	per pound
Old butter	9d	per pound
Onions	3d	per pound
Beef	5d & 5½d	per pound
Mutton	5½d & 6d	per pound
Pork	5½d	per pound
Sugar	8d	per pound
Bacon	7½d	per pound
Hay	6d	per stone

April 1795. 10th. In compliance with an order from Government to raise a man for every 70th house, the different towns returned their different quotas. They are to act as landsmen in the Navy. They gave from 20 to 30 guineas per man. The townships were trust together and Chadderton raised 3¾, Oldham 10½.

Peggy, wife of Thomas Mannocks keeper of the 'Cheshire Cheese', Oldham died.

April 1795. 5th. A Treaty of Peace concluded at Basel in Switzerland betwixt the Republic of France and the King of Prussia.

8th. The Prince of Wales married to the Princess Caroline of Brunswick, his own cousin and a party of recruits of 93rd with George Rowbottom marched on their route for Londonderry.

9th. A letter was received from Botany Bay and I am sorry to say it brings the melancholy tidings of the death of William Booth, late of . . .

. . . Royton. This person formerly resided at Royton and followed the occupation of Butcher, Fustian Manufacturer and kept the first Inn in Royton, carrying on the above business in a very extensive line. Was a sober, industrious person and was consequently a person of great credit but, when at the highest pitch of splendour and believed to be a person who by his industry to have amassed a great deal of property, Dame Fortune frowned, he became embarrased in his circumstances and in this dilemma he forged several fictitious names to Bills of Exchange. He became a bankrupt . . .

. . . to the surprise of the Country, and it being believed that a deal of fraud was practised to conceal its effects. He was taken into custody for the Fictitious Bills. In August 1788, he appeared at the Bar at Lancaster but the prosecutor did not frame a Bill against him. He was removed to York and in March 1789 was found guilty of forging these fictitious names and received sentence of death, but through the interference of his friends which were still numerous, his sentence was changed to transportation for 7 years.

April 1795. 25th. Beef sold 6 pence per pound at Oldham this day and flour 2 shillings and 6 pence per peck.

27th. A Clodding Match, Robert Ogden, commonly called "Robin O'the Quakers" at Northmoor, for a trifling wager threw a stone 165 yards one road and 185 the contrary road. 160 yards was the given length.

23rd. The trial of Warren Hastings for high crimes and misdemeanours while Governor of India concluded when he was acquitted. This trial commenced February 11th 1788 before the peers.

April 1795. It should have been mentioned in its proper place that in January last Mary, daughter of John Schofield of Top 'o th' Maggot Lane died age 20 years. Disorder a fever.

30th. Uncommon fine weather but every necessary of life advances astonishly so that the poor experience the most afflicting tortures.

May 1795. 1st. Sally, daughter of Joseph Travis of Top o' th' Moor died age 19 years. Disorder, a fever.

3rd. The Coroner took an inquest on the body of a child at Milkstone which died in consequence of drinking some boiling water out of a tea kettle spout.

2nd. Oldham Fair and a very fine day. A deal of company and at night those persons who bear the character of Jacobins were much insulted by the ignorant, impudent blaggards.

May 1795. 11th. Anna, wife of Philip Buckley died. Disorder, childbed age 27 years. They lived at Winnock and had been married only 5 weeks and Mrs. Ann Taylor, relect of the late Mr. Samual Taylor of Bottom of Northmoor.

14th. James Lees, late keeper of the 'Ring of Bells' Alehouse, Oldham died.

20th. Samuel, son of Samuel Elison of Couldhurst died. He had sometime back been attacked with palsey.

May 1795. 5th. Died off Yarmouth, Isle of Wight, James Needham, Grenadier in the 57th Regiment of Foot. He formerly resided in Maggot Lane, enlisted in January 1794. Was in Flanders in that ever-memorable Campaign. That year he had the misfortune to have his leg broke in the retreat of the combined Army and lying a long time without assistance was frostbit and was never well after. His age, 28 years.

21st. Died Mary, wife of Joseph Travis of Top o' th' Moor. The distress of this man's mind are beyond comprehension having two of his dearest connections taken of this month. Disorder, a fever, age 40 years.

May 1795. 21st. James Whitehead (son of Thomas Whitehead of Maggot Lane), private in the 12th Regiment of Foot, died at Portchester Barracks, Hampshire.

27th. Several exceedingly cold days last past. Strong frost in the mornings attended with an East wind which has greatly damaged vegetation.

29th. Died Sally, wife of James Whittaker of Cowhill, age 45 years.

May 1795. During this month, the following Regiments arrived in England from the Continent and at the following places, viz: River Thames – 1st, 2nd, 3rd Regiments of Guards; Portsmouth, Foot Regiments 12, 27, 28, 40, 54, 57, 59, 79, 80, 84; Harwich 3, 14, 19, 33, 38, 42, 53, 63, 78, 88; Newcastle-upon-Tyne 35, 37, 44, 85, 89. By letters from the above Regiments they confirm the intelligence received in the newspapers of the sufferings of the poor men, and that during the last campaign a great number were killed, wounded and taken prisoner, besides froze to death.

Heat race at Kersal Moor, Manchester, May 1780

May 1795 . . . and likewise the 87th Regiment of foot was taken prisoners at Bergen op Zoom in January last (*33).

To the surprise of all his neighbours, John Schofield of Top of Maggot Lane enlisted into the Sheffield Volunteers on Kersal Moor this day. He is upwards of 50 years of age.

May 1795. During this month the Volunteer Corps of Horse and foot received orders from Government to augment their different corps and Lord Suffields of the Norfolk Volunteers and the Lancashire fencables picked up a deal of recruits in Oldham and its environs.

Observations.

Every necessary of life advanced to an uncommon pitch and absolutely out of the reach of the lower class of poor, for it is a fact that flour is selling 2 shillings and 6 pence to 2 shillings and 8 pence per peck.

May 1795. Meal 2s to 2s 2d per peck; Mutton 6d per pound, beef 6d per pound; veal 4 1/2 to 5d per pound; lamb 8d to 10d per pound; bacon 8d per pound. Fustian weaving at the lowest pitch imaginable, hatting brisk, light goods brisk but wages low such as ginghams, calicoes, Nankeens etc. Kersalmoor Races ended on the 29th - very thinly attended. Some computed the spectators at one quarter, nay some said one half less than usual, but an uncommon deal of recruiting partys which met with but poor success. The branches of the verdant oak more free from rapine . . .

. . . and plunder for the enthusiasm of war. No peace with France and allsorts of oppression at home and the recent victorys of the French have humbled the mind of the Enthusiast so that the poor Cottager may be without oak at his door and the modest traveller may walk without a branch of it in his hat so that in Manchester this year, there was no demand for oak and last year there were several cartloads of oak branches sold and a general call for more.

June 1795. 4th. Being His Majestys birthday, it was ushered in with ringing of bells and other demonstrations of joy.

6th. New potatos sold at Manchester 3 pence per pound. At Oldham gooseberries 2 pence per quart.

8th. An absolute fact. Jonathan Jackson, Badger of Oldham, sells his flour at the price of 2 shillings and 9 pence per peck, 12lb to the peck; and meal sold 2 shillings and 1 penny per peck at Thomas Shaw's this day.

June 1795. 9th. A very high wind yesterday and this morning which injures all fruits and vegetation.

6th. George, the son of James Wood of Bullstake aged 6 years, wandered from home to the great grief of his parents, but was happily found in Manchester.

5th. Most tremendous rough this day, especially about Liverpool, Eccles, Flixton etc. where it thundered very much. It rained so that the waters rose astonishingly.

June 1795. 6th. A lamentable fact this day. Sarah, daughter of Adam Dawson of Bawtry Lane in Tonge, in consequence of some dispute with her father, put an end to her life by drowning herself near that place, her age 16 years 8 months.

> "Then crowds succeed who prodigal of breath
> Themselves anticipate the doom of death
> Tho' free from guilt they cast their lives away
> And sad and sullen hate the golden day
> Oh with what joy the wretches now would bear
> Toil and woe to breath the vital air".

June 1795. 12th. Died Mr. James Hindle, Chemist, Druggist and Apothecary, Oldham.

16th. Died far advanced in years, Betty Holden of Holdenfold.

May 1st. Mr. John Lees of Church lane paid his first payment as part of the purchase for the Lordship or Manor of Werneth. There was ringing of bells and other demonstrations of joy in the occasion. Price £30,000.

June 1795. 18th. James Barnes, weaver of Winnock very much bruised by being jammed betwixt a wall and a cartwheel at Lane End.

12th. Two of the Oxford Militia shot this day in consequence of the high price of bread. Several Regiments broke out into acts of riot and mutiny. The Oxford Militia in particular were very forward. (These disturbances happened in April and May). Two of the Oxford, Sykes and Sanson were hanged at Horsham on the 13th. 2 of the Oxford, Edward Cook and Henry Parrish were shot, several whipped.

June 1795. 9th. Death of Louis, son and heir of the late Louis 16th, King of France. Died this day in the Temple at Paris. He was born March 27th 1785.

15th. The soldiers of all Regiments received orders a few days since that they must have beef and mutton - 4½ pence per pound and bread 4lb for 5 pence - Government pays the rest.

20th. A letter received from Frank Thomson and to the inexpressible joy of his wife he is in health, contrary to the report of a letter which said he was dead, for which see page 22.

June 1795. 3rd. The City of Copenhagen in Denmark nearly destroyed by fire.

21st. The North wind still continues to blow with great velocity attended with strong frosts and last night it froze so astonish that still waters were froze over and potato wistles and other tender plants were destroyed.

23rd. A great riot at Birmingham on account of the high price of provisions. The magistrates called in the aid of the Military who fired on the mob whereby one was killed and several wounded.

June 1795. 21st. Sailbury or Old Sarum, Wiltshire, the unparalled frost which happened last night has killed several hundreds of sheep in this neighbourhood owing to there being new shorn.

25th. A lamentable misfortune as Thomas Beswick, bricklayer of Boggard hole Oldham, while repairing a chimney at Priesthill Oldham. He fell off the house and was killed on the spot.

26th. For several days past very fine rain.

Page 34

June 1795. 28th. It is with the greatest pleasure we announce that the price of weaving is considerably advancing, especially light goods. 36 Nankeens, which were wove last winter at 16 shillings per piece is now 26 shillings and other light goods in proportion. It must not be denied that strong fustian is advancing especially nine shaftcords, Jeand Thicksets, and Constitution Cords all rose 5 shillings per piece so that piece which was 40 is now 45 shillings. But to prevent the poor for being over happy every necessary of life rapidly . . .

Page 35

. . . increases. The following statement of a few articles may be depended on as a fact viz; flour 60 shillings per load, 3 shillings and a penny per peck, Jonathan Jackson sells it $3\frac{1}{2}$d per lb. There is flour at an inferior sort at 3 shillings per peck. Meal is 2s ld; cheese $5\frac{1}{2}$ and 6d per pound; bacon $8\frac{1}{2}$d per pound; old potatos 12s a load at Abraham Jackson's, Priesthill Oldham. He likewise sells potatos 13d per score. New potatos sell this day $3\frac{1}{2}$ pence per pound. Gooseberries $3\frac{1}{2}$ pence per quart.

29th. Oldham this day, Monday news arrived of Lord Bridport having on the 23rd beat the Brest fleet and taken three sail.

Page 36

July 1795.

4th. It is an absolute fact that Thomas Buckley of Burnley lane bought one peck or 12 lb of flour off Joseph Bradley of Oldham for which he gave 3 shillings and 3 pence.

9th. Mary Scoles, an elderly gentlewoman of Oldham interred this day.

10th. John Wood of Northmoor bought one twopenny loaf off John Mellow of Northmoor the weight of which was about 7 ounces and three quarters of an ounce.

Page 37

July 1795. 9th. The house of George Scoles, a bankrupt of Oldham was sold by auction, bought by James Smethurst, Landlord of 'Cotton-tree' Tavern. Price £383.

10th. Flour, sold at London 70 shillings a load. 240 lb the Quarter peck. Loaf was one shilling.

13th. Thomas Wroe, in opposition to Truth and Justice refused to pay Thomas Buckley his wages but, being brought before the magistrates at Rochdale he was there compelled to pay Buckley's demand.

20th. A cow of Simon Holdings of Holdenfold, having been bit by a mad dog was attacked with the hydrophobia, but was immediately shot.

Page 38

July 1795. 18th. Fine flour sold at Manchester this day 75 shillings per load. New potatos 10s 6d per load. At Oldham this day new potatos 2lb per penny, a fine sort a pound and half per penny.

Cock Fighting

Cock Fighting

This day a main of cocks was fought in the barn, Chadderton Hall, betwixt Sir Watts Horton Bart and Thomas Horton Esq. of Hoyrood which was won by the former.

Mark well

Joseph Milne entered as Tenants on Mr. Fawcetts factory at Top o th Moor in May last.

Page 39

A reward paid to a false tongue.

John Erington Esquire of Greys, County of Essex, having for a long time paid his addresses to a Miss Broderick on the score of marriage, shamefully deserted her and married another woman. Miss Broderick, irritated at such conduct suffered passion to surmount reason and was driven to a state of distraction. In this dilemma she went to Mr. Erington's house and with a loaden pistol shot him dead in the presence of his new bride. Miss Broderick was tried at Chelmsford Azzizes. July 1795 the Jury brought her in insane.

Page 40

July 1795. 20th. At a time when every persons wits is afloat to invent a substitute for flour the following is recommended as a composition for a pudding: (*34) Two pounds of potatos boiled, peeled and mashed. Take a pint of milk, three eggs, two ounces of moist sugar. Mix them well together and send it to the oven for three quarter of an hour.

27th. It is with heartfelt pleasure I announce that Nankeens and other light goods keep rapidly increasing. Nankeens are now 30 shillings per piece at Mr. Lees, Church Lane, Oldham.

Page 41

July 1795. 25th. At Manchester this day provisions rose so as to be nearly out of the reach of the poor. The following is a true statement of the following articles this day viz, Meal 47 shillings to 49 shillings, potatos sold 12 shillings to 18 shillings per load.

27th. At Oldham meal sells 2s 6d for 12lb, flour from 3s 6d to 4 shillings 12lb, potatos one pound and a quarter for a penny.

27th. Mad dog. In consequence of a dog of John Leans of Royly Coalpits a Shropshire man is going mad and consequently threw . . .

July 1795. . . . this neighbourhood into the greatest consternation for it appears that this dog has done a deal of damage in biting cows, horses, pigs etc. A fine milk cow of John Taylor of Holdenfold was under the necessity of being shot this morning. A horse was shot at Cinderhill a few days since that was attacked with the above malady, besides Simon Holding's cow which was shot on the 26th instant.

28th. Richard Broom, breadbaker of Oldham, conveying his loaves to Delph was met near Delph by a gang of . . .

. . . tumultuous women who emptied his caravan of the bread and sold it two pence per pound and returned Broom the money.

30th. Thomas Ogden, Muffin Baker Oldham gave 4 pounds and 10 shillings for a load of fine flour to Thomas Andrew of Edgelane.

22nd. A Treaty of Peace concluded at Basel in Switzerland betwixt the King of Spain and the Republic of France.

July 1795. Riots at Manchester, Rochdale, Oldham etc. On Thursday the 30th, owing to the uncommon price of the different necessaries of life, a large mob collected in Manchester, chiefly women and boys, and did a deal of damage by breaking windows and destroying furniture of the Corndealers and Swailers but however at evening the Lighthorse were called out of the Barracks and the mob dispersed. At Oldham the same evening a large number of women and boys collected . . .

. . . together and broke the windows of John Taylor of Primrose Bank, Richard Broom, Joseph Bradley, Robert Mayal, Abraham Jackson - all of Oldham. They retired that night after giving the above Swailers some hearty curses. These deluded people believing it to be these Swailers that caused meal to be so dear; in the morning Mr. Pickford came to Oldham and sent for a troop of lighthorse to Manchester. The horse soon arrived and a large mob again collected. The principal of the rioters of last night were apprehended and Mary Collinson, commonly called Queen Betty Garside; Mary Stott were handcuffed together.

July 1795. Edmund Standering, Joseph Ogden were handcuffed together and were conveyed to the New Bailey under a strong escort of Lighthorse. When they came near the Methodist Chapel the mobbers made a terrible attack with stones on the Military in order to rescue the prisoners. The soldiers sent for more assistance which immediately joined them and by firing their pistols and slashing away with their swords wounded several of the rioter and put their prisoners into a coach and conveyed them safe to prison and at the New Cross, Manchester this day the mob again assembled . . .

. . . and forcibly took a cartload of Meal belonging to William Watering of Waterhead Mill which they immediately divided when the Magistrates with the Light Horse again dispersed them.

Saturday August first, the mob at Oldham shewed an inclination again to mischief but Sir W. Horton, appearing at six o'clock morning, by his prudent, humane and modest discourse persuaded them to go to their homes.

On Tuesday August 4th a great number of people from Saddleworth came to Oldham and marched for the Windmill, Edgelane but then marched back and gave the Swailers to lower provisions or they would come again on Saturday.

August 1795. This caused great confusion and Sir Watts and Mr. Pickford again called the Lighthorse to their assistance.

On Thursday 6th Sir Watts Horton and Mr. Pickford called a meeting and remonstrated with the Badgers, when Sir Watts proved himself a warm advocate to the poor and the Badgers agreed to sell meal at two shillings per peck for 3 weeks next ensuing.

And on Saturday the 8th Sir Watts Horton, Mr. Pickford and about 50 especial Constables with 50 Lighthorse marched to Greenacres moor in order to meet the Saddleworth mobbers who had said they would come this day but the . . .

. . . Saddleworth people not appearing, the Magistrates dismissed the Military and the people dispersed. In all the above critical business Sir Watts Horton gained the love and the esteem of all ranks of people and by his judicious judgement and unexampled wisdom it was owing that peace and happiness being happily restored and that the same lamentable misfortuncs did not take place as took place in Rochdale, for there were riots in Rochdale, Bolton, Bury, Ashton-under-Lyne and indeed in most of towns in England.

3rd. On Monday at Rochdale owing to the dearness of provisions; meal selling at upwards of 50 shillings a load, a large number of people assembled. They were by the Magistrates repeatedly ordered to disperse but on refusal Doctor Drake (Vicar of Rochdale and a Magistrate) ordered the Rochdale fencables, commanded by John Entwhistle of Foxhole to fire, which totally killed two aged men and wounded another man in the leg and several had . . .

. . . a hairs breadth escape. The soldiers remained under arms all night but no further mischief commenced.

5th. John Taylor of Primrose Bank and sold Meal at 3 shillings per peck this week.

10th. Abraham Jackson of Oldham sold flour at four pence halfpenny per pound.

15th. Manchester Meal has sold this day 47 shillings per load but it is a fact that it sold on the first instant at from 50 shillings to 52 shillings per load.

August 1795. 22nd. Manchester the following is a true statement of the price of meal. This day old meal from 35 to 37 shillings per load. New meal from 45 to 47 shillings per load. Potatos, owing to the wetness of this week were very dear and at Oldham it is with heartfelt joy I relate that Joseph Bradley sold meal, one shilling and eleven pence per peck and flour two shillings and nine pence per peck.

Horse stealing. About the middle of last . . .

. . . month John Bates was found guilty of stealing a mare, the property of one Mr. Perkins of Somersetshire. He was pursued into Worcestershire, was tried at Worcester but the Judge reprieved before he left the City. This Bates was a Derbyshire man but had of late resided at Oldham where he had a fair character, but being a little embarrassed in debt fled into Wiltshire for refuge where he was weak enough to commit the above deed.

25th. Bought two pecks of Malt off Mrs.Whittaker, price 1s 10d per peck, weight 18lb 8 oz, hops 4 oz 3d.

Manchester Market Place

Page 54

24th. Being Middleton Rushbearing Monday it was very throngly attended and owing to Nankeens and other light goods being so high in wages the inhabitants appeared in high spirits and well dressed. There were seven rushcarts on Saturday.

26th. Joy appears in every countenance on the rapid fall of Meal and Flour.

and last night Jane, daughter of Jonathan Chadwick of Wood got out of bed asleep, fell downstairs and was much bruised.

Page 55

August 1795. 29th. Manchester this day new meal sold 42 shillings per load, old meal 35 to 37 shillings per load.

And Oldham Rushbearing commenced and there were four rushcarts viz; one from Cowhill, one from Nimblenook near Denton, one from Hollins, one from Fog-lane and owing to the fineness of the weather there were an uncommon deal of people. On Sunday a finer day never came from heaven. Oldham uncommon throng and a deal of strangers which in . . .

Page 56

. . . general were well dressed.

Monday 31st. Rushbearing Monday. The sky serene and clear. Not a cloud to be seen. Very warm and a fine modest breeze of air. An uncommon deal of people in general, two nymphs to one swain, the war having drained these towns of men so that, but one recruiting party appeared which was the Windsor Forresters Horsemen dressed in green. The poor people faired better than they have done at the Rushbearings of 1793 and 1794, for all sorts of business brisk except strong Fustians.

Page 57

September 1795. 5th. Manchester this day new meal sold from thirty six to thirty eight shillings per load. Old meal from 30 to 35 shillings per load. Potatos, owing to the fineness of the weather the farmers being engaged in cutting their corn, were scarce and dear.

9th. Archery. Lady Horton's quiver of arrows were shot for in the park and won by Mr. Thackery. The day being fine there was a large assemblange of ladies and gentlemen and an uncommon deal of spectators.

Harvesting

Page 58

September 1795. 12th. Manchester this day new meal sold from 38 to 40 shillings a load. Old from 30 to 37 shillings per load. At Oldham new meal 2 shillings and 1 penny per peck; old very good 1 shilling and 10 pence per peck. Flour 3 shillings to 3 shillings and 6 pence per peck.

August 28th. Peace concluded betwixt the Republic of France and the Landgrave of Hesse-Cassel (*35).

Page 59

September 1795. 13th. An account was received a few weeks since from the West Indies giving account of the death of James Henthorn and Dan Prestwich, both of the 34th Regiment of foot.

14th. The rapid demands for Nankeens surpasses anything ever heard of before so that most of the strong fustian weavers are turned to that business.

16th. Accident happened at Royton. A son of Joseph Buckley's aged 9 years who drove a horse at a factory, there being jammed betwixt Tailpole and wall, was killed.

Page 60

September 1795. In this month great mutinies in Ireland in the 104th or Manchester Volunteers, 105, 111, 173 - on account of these Regiments being drafted into other Regiments and sent to the West Indies.

18th. John Mills, commonly called 'Little Britain', leg broke and much bruised in a Coalpit at Back of Edge. He died March 9th 1796.

Page 61

September 1795. 19th. Manchester this day new meal sold from 40 to 42 shillings per load, old same as last Saturday, potatos cheap and at Oldham new meal sold 2 shillings and 2 pence per peck.

20th. A letter from John Kay of the 12th of foot, but late of Busk states that he is drafted out of the 12th Regiment. Is invalided and ordered for Gibralter.

21st. British Heroism. James Buckly, late of Beartrees has 6 sons which are as follows; John now in Germany in the Oxford Blues . . .

. . . Joseph in the 16th Dragoons now near Newcastle-upon-Tyne; James a sailor with Lord Bridport now off the coast of France. The three others were too young to be in the King's Service. James Buckly the father now in the 93rd of foot at Kinsdale but under orders for the West Indies.

21st. Rushbearing at Duckenfield. This day there was one rushcart which was richly decorated. There were plenty of company. They have not had a Rushcart since the year 1776 except this.

September 1795. 21st. Owing to the fineness of the season the Cockcrow was seen this day and was heard to sing on the 12th instant. The above is related by persons whose characters will bear the strictest scrutiny.

22nd. Colonel William Radcliffe of Mills Bridge near Huddersfield died. His great property devolved to Mr. Pickford of Royton.

24th. Old Tommy Raynor of Old Clarks died age 85 years.

September 1795. 26th. Manchester this day, New Meal from 44 to 46 shillings per load and flour rather advanced.

30th. The following Regiments are now at Portsmouth under order for the West Indies viz: the 2nd, 3rd, 8th, 19th, 25th, 29th, 31st, 33rd, 38th, 42nd, 44th, 48th, 53rd, 55th, 63rd, 92nd Regiments of foot 22nd, 29th of Lighthorse.

October 1795. 3rd. This day attended Manchester Market and the following is the price of different articles viz: New Meal from 40 to 42 shillings per load; Flour 60 to 63 shillings per load; potatos 5 to 6 shillings per load, beef from 4 pence to 5 pence per pound, mutton ditto; pork ditto; Apples 18 pence to 22 pence per peck; Nuts 2 pence per Quart; Damson plums 3 pence per Quart and at Oldham New Meal sold 2 shillings and 1 penny per peck; Old 1 shilling and 10 pence per peck.

10th. At Manchester this day Meal, Flour nearly same as last Saturday.

October 1795. 17th. Manchester this day New meal sold from 38 to 40 shillings per load; old from 35 to 37 shillings per load.

19th. This day at Oldham new meal 2 shillings per peck, Old 1 shilling and 10 pence per peck; mutton 4½ and 5 pence per pound; beef 4 pence and 4½ pence per pound. Candles are 9 pence per pound – brown or white soap 9 pence per pound; flour 2 shillings and 6 pence to 3 shillings per peck.

14th. Oldham Fair this day much company and a deal of business.

October 1795. 20th. At Marsden this day, a large quantity of flour which was coming to Oldham was seized by the mob and sold at an abated price.

14th. The Sessions commenced at Manchester when no Bills were found against the Oldham Rioters. See page 45.

24th. Manchester this day the Meal, Flour, Potatos same as last Saturday and at Oldham the same.

October 1795. Fine weather which begun August 25th and continued 'til October.

7th, the space of 43 days which was the finest Harvest ever known. The air was very warm and at some times was very sultry and hot. All sorts of insects and reptiles as if a second summer was commenced and the earth seemed as if she sent forth a double portion of vegetation. The Brooks, for lack of rain, were low and the fishes as sportive and active as if in June or July. The birds . . .

. . . by the uncommonness of the weather joined all products of Nature with the melodious notes which would have convinced the most rigid atheist of the Blessings of the Almighty God; it should not be forgot that fleas were very numerous and very much annoyed poor people in bed i'th night.

31st. At Manchester this day New Meal sold from 40 to 43 shillings per load and at Oldham 2 shillings and 2 pence per peck and this day died Sarah, wife of Isaac Hardy of Winnock. Disorder a consumption.

October 1795. Martha relict of the late James Ashton of Wood died.

29th. Thursday, the Parliament meet when his Majesty's speech was inclinable to war. The Ministry had a majority in the House of Commons of 180. His Majesty in passing to the Parliament House was grossly insulted by a mob of 150,000 who broke the carriage windows to pieces, they continually crying "Give us peace, give us bread, down with Pitt", etc.

November 1795. 5th. Great bonfires and other demonstrations of joy.

7th. Manchester this day, Meal sold from 43 to 45 shillings per load, flour 62 shillings per load, potatos from 5 to 6 shillings per load.

At Oldham, Meal sold from 2 shillings and 2 pence to 2 shillings and 4 pence per peck.

Potatos, notwithstanding the very great crop of potatos to owners in this neighbourhood gave over selling before they were all got up and are reserving them for Spring when they hope the price will be much raised - what they have sold - the price is William Royle at Beartrees 6 shillings and 8 pence.

William Royle of Beartrees 6s 8d per load, Robert Smith 6 shillings per load, but that oracle of oppression Mrs.Alice Walker of Burnley Lane sold hers 8 shillings per load. Their crops were very large and uncommon good ones.

12th. The following is a true statement of the price of the following articles viz: Treacle 5 pence per pound, Candles 11 pence per pound, Soap 10 pence per pound, Fustian Weaving low, Nankeens brisk and wages high. For the 36 reed 29 shillings.

November 1795. 12th. Nanny, daughter of Mary Wrigley, Keeper of the Red Lion Inn Oldham was interred this day.

14th. Manchester this day Meal and Flour exactly as last Saturday Potatos from 5 to 6 shillings a load.

12th. Died James Clegg of Wood age 39 years, disorder consumption.

21st. Manchester this day, Meal sold from 40 to 45 sillings per load, potatos 6 shillings per load, Flour 62 shillings per load.

November 1795. 25th. Died this day Mary wife of Thomas Kay of Old Clarks aged 74 years and John Buckley, shoemaker of Oldham age 77 years and Hardman the Collier who was so miserably burnt with the fire damp near Royley fold, died this day.

30th. Treacle sells five pence half penny per pound.

28th. Manchester this day Meal sold from 40 to 42 shillings per load.

December 1795. 5th. Manchester this day Meal sold from 40 to 42 shillings, flour 62 shillings, potatos 6 shillings, Mutton 5 pence, Beef 5 pence, Pork 6 pence per pound. Nankeens dropped to 28 shillings per piece and the same day Samuel Fletcher opened his new alehouse in Oldham Lane near Mumps as did Simon Mellow, his house near Royton; and James Kay, his house on the New Road some time since. They were all three licenced the last September.

6th. James Lees, Badger, Maggot-lane sells Meal two shillings and four pence per peck, Treacle 5 pence halfpenny per lb.

December 1795, November 30th, this day at the Angel Inn Oldham, Mellor's estate Sun-field near Edge-lane was sold for £1000 and John Taylor of Primrose-bank was the purchaser. Likewise the auction of near 400 volumes of books of Mr. Pickford's begun selling by auction at Oldham.

12th. This day at Manchester the price of provisions nearly same as last Saturday.

16th. Wife of James Mellor, Blacksmith and Innkeeper died age 45 years. Disorder Consumption and of Edge Lane.

December 1795. 7th. Petitions against the seditious meeting Bill and the Bill for the better preserving his Majesty's person were signed by great numbers at Manchester where there was a meeting for the purpose and a petition for peace by the same party, the above petitions signed by great numbers in Bolton, Stockport, Oldham, Royton, etc. The opposite party under their old shield of Church & King vehemently opposed them, proving in a petition that the above Bills might pass into law.

19th. Manchester this day Meal and potatos same as last Saturday. Flour some lower.

December 1795. 23rd. This day Mary Wrigley's furniture and stock in trade were sold by auction at her house the Red Lion Inn, Oldham.

26th. Manchester this day Meal, flour and potatos same as last Saturday. Oldham Meal 2 shillings and 2 pence per peck, flour 2s and 10 pence per peck, potatos 7 pence per score, beef 5 pence per pound, mutton 5 pence halfpenny per pound, candles 8 pence per pound.

About this time Edmund Whittaker of the 'Hare and Hounds' entered as a tenant on the Red Lion Inn Oldham.

December 1795. 28th. In Chadderton, this the great main of Cocks betwixt Sir Watts Horton, Smith, Feeder and William Bamford Esquire. Butterworth, Feeder was fought here when Mr. Bamford won 8 mains out of 11 and 3 byes out of 4. There was a deal of Company and much betting.

31st. A fine day and the year near its end and the finest weather since the middle of November ever seen, which makes the situation of poor more happy. There is a greater appearance of a plentiful Christmas . . .

Page 80

. . . than has been for some years past for notwishstanding the high price of provisions, by the mere dint of Industry the poor are at this time decently stocked for the Chistmas week.

The End

1797 (all entries for the year 1796 are missing)

January 1797. The year 1797 commenced on a Sunday which was a moderate fine day and what by industry and economy the poor were moderately supplied with Christmas cheer and notwithstanding the dearness of some of the necessarys of life and the lowness of work, the ancient hospitality has peeped from behind the dark clouds of adversity for it is observable that there has been more suppering nights, by one . . .

. . . neighbour giving a treat to another than has been for some time.

7th. Wife of Jeptha Garlick of Burnley lane died. Disorder a violent fever.

15th. Wife of Graves at Burnley lane interred. Disorder a consumption.

14th. Ann, wife of Benjamin Woolstoner of Maygate Lane died. She had been a long time afflicted with a palsey.

John Law, Constable of Royton died. Disorder Consumption.

30th. The weather for several weeks past has been uncommon fine and very much resembles Spring.

The lots for the Supplementary Militia were drawn at Middleton for the Hundred of Salford. Oldham quota 89, Chadderton 29, Royton 30, Crompton 29. The whole for Lancashire is 5150 men. Substitutes were obtained from 4 to 10 guineas. (*36)

January 1797. The following is a true statement of the prices of the following articles viz.

	Shilling	*pence*			*Shilling*	*pence*	
Meal	1	4	per peck	Candles		9½	per pound
Flour	1	8	per peck	Cheese		6 to 7	per pound
Very good	1	9	per peck	Pork		6 to 7	per pound
Manchit Flour	2	0	per peck	Beef		6 to 7	per pound
Malt	1	8	per peck	Mutton		6 to 7	per pound
Treacle		5½	per pound	Potatos		6½	per score
Butter		9	per pound	Onions		2	per pound

February 1797. 2nd. Daniel Knott of Fog-lane died age 74 years. Disorder, a palsey. A person of a peaceable disposition of mind and a devout Christian.

18th. The frost which commenced on the 13th still continues but is remarkably fine.

20th. Uncommon good Meal sold at 15 pence per peck at the Warehouse, Oldham.

18th. Middleton this evening, as Robert Taylor was crossing the road, just as two carts were passing, the one endeavouring to pass the other, one of the horses trod him down, the wheel run over his head and . . .

. . . killed him on the spot. The Jury sat two days and brought in their verdict Manslaughter against the Carter, who of course was committed to Lancaster Castle but at the assizes was acquitted.

21st. All kinds of weaving uncommon low. Plain Nankeen which 15 months ago were 15 shillings per cut are now wove for ten shillings per cut two yards longer. Twill and plain Nankeen which was 5 pence per yard is now but three pence halfpenny and . . .

. . . all sorts of light goods in proportion. Fustians lower every day but there is one great happiness, namely the rapid fall of allsorts of grain.

25th. Uncommon fine weather and every appearance of a forward Spring.

28th. This day the Supplementary Militia for Manchester were swore in at the New Bailey. Substitutes in general fetched from 6 to 10 Guineas per man.

March 1797. 3rd. Rochdale this day the Supplementary Militia were swore in here. Substitutes fetched from 6 to 8 Guineas per man and one Thomas Tetlow, a constable for Chadderton found guilty of making false lists in numbering for the Supplementary Militia by screening his son; was by the Magistrates fined 5 pounds but was mitigated to 40 shillings.

4th. John Butterworth, commonly called 'Jack o'th'orders' was . . .

. . . for stripping a Clothes Edge near Glodwick, committed to the New Bailey.

2nd. John Walwork, joiner and carpenter died in consequence of the wounds received on the 28th February last, by a piece of wood falling on him. He was an elderly man.

7th. Joseph Buckley (son of James Buckley, formerly of Busk) died. This young man, about 4 years ago entered into the 16th Regiment of Light Dragoons. Being of a delicate habit and being confined in camps and barracks brought on a consumption. Age 21 years. He died at Bullstake near Alderroot.

March 1797. 8th. Was observed a general fast through England and Wales.

11th. At Oldham this day Meal sold 13 pence per peck, excellent good, 14 ditto, Flour 21 pence a peck, Malt 17 pence a peck.

13th. Uncommon cold frosty weather and has been so for several days. The wind north east.

11th. Manchester this day potatos sold 3 shillings and 9 pence per load, Meal 21 shillings, Flour 36 shillings a load.

March 1797. 18th. New warehouse Oldham, this day good meal sold 13 pence per peck, flour 20 pence per peck, Old butter scarce and dear and selling single pounds at 10 pence.

22nd. Thomas Jackson of Priesthill Oldham interred in the new burying ground, Methodist Chapel.

Victorys obtained last month. February 14th Admiral Sir John Jervis with 15 sail of the line defeated the Spanish fleet of 27 sail of the line. On the 18th Admiral Harvey and Sir Ralph Abercromby captured . . .

. . . the island of Trinidad – took one 74-gun ship and the enemy burnt an 84 and two 74-gun ships to prevent them falling into the hands of the English and the victorious General Bonapart at the head of the invincible Republicans totally defeated the Austrian army and captured the impregnable city of Mantua.

30th. Meal sells at Oldham 15 pence, Flour 21 pence a peck, butter 10½ pence per pound.

25th. James Collier of Northmoor opened . . .

. . . his 'hush house' viz selling malt liquor without a licence.

31st. Fine weather and has been for some days past. Some days before the fine weather commenced it was very frosty and cold.

All sorts of weaving very bad especially light goods such as Nankeens which were wove for 9 shillings a cut. Calicoes were wove as low as half a crown a cut.

April 1797. 21st. Ended the great Main of cocks at Manchester betwixt Sir Watts Horton of Chadderton and Sir Rowland Wynne of Nostle near Wakefield which was won by Sir Watts.

25th. No material alteration on the price of provisions since the last statement. And, David Jackson of Oldham, Hardwareman, interred this day.

Ashton-under-Lyne, March 26th. Yesterday evening George Berkenshaw and his wife were found with their throats cut in a shocking manner. The woman was dead and the man expiring. It appeared they have lived very disagreeable together and that the man had cut the woman's throat first and in order to screen himself from the law cut his own. They were both buried in Ashton Churchyard.

29th. Beef and Mutton each sold 7 pence a pound and old butter $10^1/_2$ per pound. 36 Reed Nankeen, 49 yards long wove for 9 shillings.

May 1797. 1st. Peter Whitehead, son of Mr.Edmund Whitehead, hatter, Oldham interred this day.

7th. Last night an uncommon cold stormy night and a deal of snow on the hills this morning. For several days past it has been uncommon cold and a deal of chilly rain which makes it an uncommon late Spring.

11th. Yesterday was one of the most tremendous days for wind, rain and snow ever remembered by the old person living. The wind North East, and this day the wind very high with sleet and rain.

May 1797. 12th. This day has been an uncommon cold wet day, the surface of the Earth soft and dirty as in the middle of December, the air full of clouds and watery vapours, the air very cold and piercing. Vegetation and Spring have not yet made much appearance.

15th. With great happiness we announce that cold wet weather is terminated, for yesterday was an uncommon warm day.

May 1797. The victorious General Napoleon Bonaparte was born in Corsica in 1767 (a work was published in 1799 which states him to have been born in 1769).

By a return made to the war office it appears that there has died in the last 12 months in St. Domingo only; 362 British Officers, 7374 privates. This account was taken from the *Manchester Gazette*, May 13th 1797.

16th. Heavy loud cracks and vivid flashes of lightning.

20th. Last night uncommon loud cracks of thunder with most tremendous flashes of lightning.

May 1797. 24th. An uncommon fine day so there is a great change of weather.

28th. The weather is again turned to very wet and cold.

29th Was observed as a day of joy by the Church and King. People who, to testify their loyalty put up oak branches at their doors and the other party rigidly forbearing to deck their doors which caused great contention betwixt the partys.

31st. Still cold wet weather but there is plenty of grass.

June 1797. 3rd. The cold wet weather still continues to the great detriment of vegetation for the air is continually cold and mostly rainy.

4th. Kings birthday but being Sunday, was observed on Monday with great pomp and festivity.

9th. Manchester Races concluded and notwithstanding the wetness of the roads they were attended by an immense concourse of people of both sexes. On Wednesday it rained all day and at about two o'clock afternoon it fell such a hailstorm as was seldom . . .

. . . ever seen at any season. Very few soldiers and but a very few recruiting parties attended.

13th. The wet weather attended with uncommon cold still continues.

20th. Last night an uncommon cold boisterous night and still continues with rain and piercing wind.

14th. This morning died at Nathanroe Oldham, Nathan Barlow hatter.

21st. Uncommon cold boisterous day.

22nd and 23rd. Very cold wet days so that the crops begin to mourn.

June 1797. Oldham 23rd. Last night or early this morning the shop of Henry Harrison Draper and Habberdasher was broke open and robbed of a considerable sum of money. Diligent search is making after the depradaters of this wickedness.

25th. The weather is much changed and from severe wet and cold is turned to moderate warmth.

19th. This day the Supplementary Cavalry were swore in at Middleton when substitutes went from 5 to 10 guineas each. This was an order of Government and the conditions were that every person who kept . . .

June 1797. . . . a Saddle Horse was to be numbered and where the Townships did not contain ten horses of this description, townships were thrown together and classed into tens and lots drawn. One out of every ten which lotted person was to find a man and a horse to be exercised for twenty one days but all the class was at equal expense with and same as the lotted person.

30th. Uncommon cold, wet weather such as was never known before by the oldest person living.

June 1797. About the beginning of May a most dangerous Mutiny broke out in his Majestys fleet which lasted 'til the middle of June when the different crews returned to their duty and delivered up their delegates who were immediately tried by a Court Martial, when Richard Parker their head delegate, and several others received sentence of death and were executed.

Observations - The rainy weather which still continues is very alarming and much alarms the farmers and others, for where the ground is low and wet it but . . .

. . . promises a light crop and the Earth and air are so cold that what grass is cut, it remains in a spoiling state for want of sun and fair weather. It is allowed by the oldest persons living that such a wet Spring and thus far of a summer was never known before.

Fustian weaving is becoming exceedingly brisk and masters are beating up in all directions for weavers but in consequence of the high price of cotton, the wages are but little advanced. Cotton common for weaving Velveteens, Thicksets etc. is selling at two shillings a pound. All sorts of light goods are very low.

July 1797. 4th. Died Sarah, wife of George Rowbottom of Hollinwood age 73 years.

6th. The wet weather still continues and is extremely cold last night and this morning it rained with the greatest velocity so that the Earth was covered with water.

8th. The rainy weather still continues. Yesterday the sun shone for about four hours with spendour which induced several persons to break their hay etc. when about four o'clock it began to rain very much.

9th. The weather begins to mend and puts on a better appearance.

July 1797. 12th. The Fustian weaving begins to mend to the general joy of the poor weavers.

15th. The weather continues very good yesterday, was an extraordinary good Hay Day.

8th. Died Abraham Dronesfield of Hollinwood, formerly of Brunley Brow Northmoor. Disorder consumption, age 31 years.

18th. This day as well as the 16th and 17th have been excessive hot and good Hay Days.

19th. A good Hay Day and very hot.

July 1797. 22nd. The very fine hay weather still continues to the joy of everyone.

New potatos owing to the coldness of the Spring have been scarce and dear and are now selling at one penny per pound the finest sort, but owing to the reasonableness of the price of flour few new potoatos were used.

15th. Wife of Henry Harrison, Mercer and Draper, Oldham, interred this day.

July 1797. The Trials of the Mutineers still continues and a great number have been executed.

24th. On Monday the author of these memoirs very narrowly escaped the Fangs of Death but through the interposition of the Almighty God, miraculously escaped.

26th. Excellent fine weather and new potatos sold one pound and a Quarter for a penny.

28th. The weather is again turned to wet and cold.

25th. Died Ann, wife of Joseph Parr, Inn Holder, Streetbridge. She had been for a long time afflicted having the use of her legs taken.

July 1797. 30th. An uncommon boisterous stormy day with loud cracks of thunder. At Bury there was an uncommon hailstorm which broke a deal of windows and did other damage.

30th. Died George Rowbottom of Hollinwood, originally of Hunt Lane, Blacksmith age 65 years.

The weather for several days past has been wet and stormy attended with a deal of thunder and lightening which did a deal of damage.

August 1797. 6th. Being Sunday as is customary, though a very bad habit.

George Metcalfe, Hatter of Oldham was drowned in a pit near Bent with imprudently going past his depth.

1st. This day nine of the Mutineers were executed on board their respective ships lying near Sheerness.

14th. A very wet night last.

17th. An uncommon fine day as was two of the last.

August 1797. The beginning of this month died at Edinburgh Thomas Peter Legh Esquire of Golbourn near Warrington and of Lyme in Cheshire, Member of Parliament for Newton, Lancashire and Colonel of the Lancashire Light Dragoons.

18th. Great storm of Thunder, lightning and rain begun this morning about six o'clock which was tremendous behind expression. The cracks of thunder were awfully loud. The lightning very expressive . . .

. . . and came oftner in the course of a minute than was ever remembered before. One James Andrew was killed with lightning near Lees, and the waters in consequence of the uncommon raining rose astonishingly high - swept everything before it that fell in its way at Middleton.

A son of Abraham Harrison's Keeper of the Suffield Arms, there whilst viewing the rapidity of the stream fell into the water and notwithstanding in the presence of a great number of people was drowned. He was found in the . . .

. . . afternoon about one mile below Middleton after the water had abated. His father was present when he fell into the water and was an unhappy spectator of the above catastrophe. He was betwixt nine and ten years of age.

22nd. Saddleworth this day a great number of people attended at a place called Raven Stones in Greenfield for the purpose of blowing up by gunpowder a venerable large stone called one of the Raven Stones, which stone was situated upon a very high and lofty rock.

When the people were mining under the stone in order to lay their powder the stone suddenly fell down and made its way down a large precipice where a great number of spectators were assembled. Happily there was but one man killed but a great number were much wounded in its way to the water which runs down Greenfield. Its velocity and weight were so great that it crushed the smaller stones and levelled the ground so much that it resembled a new boldered road.

The following was taken from the *Manchester Gazette* of August 19th 1797. The National Debt of Great Britain is £409,665,570. Yearly interest . . . £16,272,597. Expense of the war for last year . . . £62,357,312.

August 1797. 26th. Being Oldham Rushbearing Saturday and a fine day was very fully attended and owing to the briskness of the Fustian business there were eight rushcarts.

On Sunday a fine day and a deal of foreigners and high spending of money.

On Monday a fine day and very throng and five Rushcarts which was a thing uncommon. There was plenty of brewing with familys which a short time since were very poor. Besides, notwithstanding the exhorbitant price of . . .

. . . Butchers meat there was plenty of beef and cabbage, and joy appeared in every countenance.

In this month there has been an uncommon deal of bilberries which sold from four to five pence per Quart.

31st. Uncommon wet weather and every appearance of it damaging the crops.

September 1797. 12th. Uncommon wet cold weather and has been so long time which causes grain and potatos to be dearer for it is a real fact that potatos sold this day at Manchester Market, ten shillings a load.

16th. Manchester this day potatos sold ten shillings a load, flour something dearer than has been of late. Meal rather higher - it sold old twenty five shillings, new thirty shillings a load.

18th. This morning died Mr. John Lees, cotton manufacturer of Pit Bank near Oldham, a gentleman of fair character.

September 1797. 14th. Chadderton this day the Archers commenced their shooting in the park here. The prize the quiver of arrows given by Lady Horton. It was a wet cold stormy day, few company and few archers and very few spectators.

19th. Fustians dropped in value, four shillings per piece this day at Manchester when the Masters immediately reduced the wages and common weaving cotton sold two shillings and sixpence a pound.

Apples are selling half a crown a peck which have lately sold at three shillings and sixpence a peck.

September 1797. Metzlaer Germany 19th yesterday died in the 30th year of his age the heroic and virtuous general Lazerous Hoche, one of the French Republican Generals. His character as a General and as a citizen surpasses any ecomiums that can be passed on him.

30th. Manchester this day the Market was full of every article of life but in consequence of the wetness of the season some articles are very dear such as Damson plums which are selling ten pence per Quart. Onions five farthings.

September 1797. Per pound turnips up as high as nine pence per peck. Old Joseph Mellor, schoolmaster of Winnook died on the 24th of this month.

Potatos this year are but a slender crop and the price consequently high in the market. They are sold from six to seven shillings a load. The farmers in this neighbourhood have but few to part with and those they sell from seven to eight shillings a load. The wetness of the season is attributed to be the cause in the failure in the crop of potatos.

October 1797. 7th. Died after lingering in the greatest agonies but yet supporting it with Christian fortitude Betty, daughter of Josua Taylor of Bottom of Northmoor. She was about 20 years of age, had been afflicted with white swellings for upwards of 2 years.

11th. Died wife of John Ogden of Bottom of Maygate Lane age about 23 years, disorder consumption.

11th. Oldham Fair, a deal of company and an uncommon deal of swine.

October 1797. 18th. The different Sick Club Societys at Oldham held their annual Feast this day and the

Rev. Mr. Winter preached an excellent sermon on the occasion.

11th. One of the most bloody and gallant engagements ever fought took place near Camperton (*37) in Holland betwixt the English fleet consisting of 16 Sail of the Line besides frigates etc. and the Dutch fleet of the same number, but fewer guns and lighter metal when the Dutch were totally defeated and lost 11 ships but 2 sunk before they got into the British ports.

The English fleet was commanded by Admiral Duncan, the Dutch fleet by Admiral DeWinter.

18th. A general illumination took place in Oldham on Duncan's victory.

At Manchester on the 20th they illuminated as they did at different days in most of town in Great Britain.

17th. A peace ratified and concluded betwixt the Republic of France and the Emperor of Germany at Udina. The Armistice for this peace was concluded the 18th of April last.

November 1797. 1st. Died Betty, wife of Joseph Scofield of Top o'th'Moor. Disorder a consumption.

5th. Bonfires, Ringing of Bells and other demonstrations of joy.

6th. Died Molly, relect of the late Josuah Winterbottom, Keeper of the Red Lion in Oldham.

11th. It has been uncommon fine for several days past and so remarkable warm that Wheelers Manchester Chronicle of the 12th instant says that it was as warm as in June.

26th. The frost which commenced a few days since broke this morning.

November 1797. 30th. Last night was one of the most tremendous nights for snow and wind ever remembered. It continued most of this day. The Mail Coach from London to Manchester was detained for thirteen hours. The weather is remarkable for being changeable, some days freezing and some days thawing and some days rainy.

The most remarkable occurance at this time is the fall of Butcher's meat which is owing to the large number of pigs which are now passing . . .

. . . in to Market besides most of familys are possessed of a good pig and never was there such a number of those useful animals before. Beef now sells at Oldham from four pence halfpenny to five pence halfpenny per pound. Mutton the same, pork from four pence to six pence per pound and that branch of the hat manufactary called ruffing or plating is entirely given up so that a large number of hands are entirely without work and Winter and want approaching makes a dismal appearance.

November 1797. 16th. Died Frederick William, King of Prussia. He was born September 25th 1744, Frederick William his son and successor born August 3rd 1770.

29th. It is with heartfelt concern that we have again to announce that the most distressing and calamitous times are again making their appearance in this unhappy country, for all sorts weaving is on the lowest ebb. Nankeen which sometime back cut such a conspicuous figure is now . . .

. . . totally annihilated. All other sorts of light goods are very low. Fustians cotton rises in price, is now selling common weaving cotton at from 2 shillings and 4 pence to 25 and 7 pence a pound. The wages of a velveteen is 10 shillings lower than three months since and all others in proportion. Hatting. Within the last month is fallen nearly to nothing for it is an absolute fact that a deal of hatters are at this time entirely without work and gloomy, as the alternative maybe several are begun of weaving fustian.

December 1797.

6th. A servant of James Taylor's of Sarah-moor having set down fifteen pounds of cotton cardings at a shop door in Oldham, while she did a small errand, they were in an instant stolen away and no trace left behind.

But be it spoken to the shame of the persons concerned in it that in this enlightened age that ignorance and superstition had such influence over them that they consulted all the witches, conjurers and wizards in this neighbourhood, but be it spoken to their disgrace these dark oracles laid the scandal on . . .

. . . an innocent person, as will appear hereafter for on the 11th John Robinshaw of Thorp was apprehended and his house searched when a quantity of Cardings which are believed to be those stolen, were found in his house. He was, of course, committed to the New Bailey to take his trial at the next sessions.

18th. Yesterday was an uncommon day for rain so that the waters rose astonishingly and did a deal of damage.

December 1797. 19th. Was observed as a day of general thanks to Almighty God for the glorious victorys obtained on the seas over our different enemies, when the colours taken by Lords Howe, Bridport, St. Vincent and Duncan were carried to St. Pauls in procession before the King, Queen, Royal Family, Great Officers of State etc. The people in general saluted His Majesty but when Mr. Pitt came nothing was heard but hisses and groans. His servants . . .

. . . were much pelted with dirt and etc. When service was concluded Mr. Pitt eluded the vigilance of the mob by going into another carriage and so got safe into Downing Street.

The effigy of Pitt was hung up in several parts of London but the mob were very civil. Opposite the Bank a Britannia was fixed up with these lines:

> "A vessel quite crazy and almost a wreck
>   At her helm as a pilot unskilled on the deck
>   Without chart or compass who ne'er heaves the lead
>   who steers by his stars or false lights in his head
>   The storm too increasing midst sholes and mids shelves
>   Half the crew in despair making rafts for themselves
>   Provisions all out, the last'water cask staved
>   By a miracle only that ship can be saved".

At Oldham etc. it was observed with great solemnity.

December 1797. 27th. Ned Lee apprehended on a charge of stealing glass from Mrs. Hibbert's Stock lane, brought before Sir Watts Horton and by him committed to the New Bailey, to take his trial for the same.

26th. Died the great patriot who put a stop to General Warrants, John Wilkes Esquire FRS, in the 72nd year of his age, died at London.

This year concludes with the most distressing times ever experienced by the oldest person living in respect of weaving and hatting being down.

FINIS

1799 (all entries for the year 1798 are missing)

Page 1

The year 1799 commenced on Tuesday which was a cold frosty day and it ushered in such a Christmas as was never experienced before, for it is impossible fully to describe the wretchedness of the poor of this once happy country, for by the lowness of the Fustian Trade, Roast beef, pies and ale are not to be seen on the poor man's . . .

Page 2

. . . table, on the contrary, it is graced with misery and want and a universal lowness of spirits and dejected countenance appear in everyone. Humanity is fled from the breast of everyone so that the wretched and miserable poor by pining - pitied and unnoticed. Oh that this New Year may be a more comfortable year than the last is my wish. There is hopes but no assurance, for things grow every day . . .

Page 3

. . . worse and worse. Nothing is to be seen or heard but the woeful tale of the poor Fustian weavers who are relating their woeful stories to one another, for by the dearness of cotton the Masters are compelled to pay the weavers a very little. Very few pieces now are paid above twelvepenny and those must be very good pieces, but most of weaving is done . . .

Page 4

. . . at nine penny. Nankeen is wove 36 reed, 50 yards long at nine shillings a cut; calicoes at 3s and 6 pence and 4 shillings a cut - 28 yards. Cotton such as is wove into velveteens, Nine shafts etc. is sold at the amazing price of 2 shillings and 10 pence a pound.

The following is an accurate statement of the price of the different articles following viz:

Grey boiling peas 2½ to 3 pence per Quart.

Page 5

Meal from	1s	6d	per peck	Butter new		11d	per pound
ditto	1s	8d	per peck	Cheese		5d to 6d	per pound
ditto very good	1s	9d	per peck	Pork		3½ to 4½	per pound
Flour very good	2s	0d	per peck	Beef		5d	per pound
ditto	1s	11d	per peck	Mutton		5d	per pound
ditto	1s	7d	per peck	Onions		1½d	per pound
ditto	1s	1d	per peck	Hops	1s	10d	per pound
Malt	1s	7d	per peck	Bacon		7d	per pound
Treacle		5½d	per pound	Soap white or Butter old		9d	per pound
Butter old		9d	per pound	Candles		8½d	per pound

Page 6

January 1799.

Potatos   5½d per score

or   9d per stroke

Salt   3d per pound

Sugar   9 to 10d per pound

1st. Joseph Wright of Old Sarah Moor died. Disorder consumption.

5th. Ann, wife of Thomas Ogden of Burnley Lane died. She had been sick a long time, age 74.

8th. Ann, wife of Eley Dyson of Chadderton Mill interred at Oldham age 71 years.

January 1799. 19th. John Scott, Hatter, Oldham died.

28th. A very keen frost commenced last night.

Through the Minister's determination on war there is very much recruiting all over England for the different Regiments; in Oldham the Lancashire Volunteers commanded by Lord Grey De Wilton and the Norfolk Volunteers . . .

. . . commanded by the Honorable William Ashton Harbord, son of Lord Suffield beat up in great style and in consequence of badness of trade picked up a great deal of recruits.

31st. The frost still continues with unabating severity and yesterday it was an uncommon day of wind and snow and this morning it is most tremendously rough.

The Fustian trade still continues very bad and the frost and snow being so against the poor it makes their situation the more deplorable, for indeed at this time they are the most miserable beings upon Earth.

February 1799. 1st. Yesterday the wind was very high and at night it begun to snow.

2nd. Yesterday the first of February was one of the most tremendous rough days ever remembered. The wind was astonishingly high and the air was darkened with . . .

. . . snow so that the valleys were soon filled which rendered the roads impassible. The Mail from London to Manchester was stopped for several days. It froze with unabating fury so that John Taylor of Primrose Bank, Oldham amongst others, had a mare froze to death on the Ripponden Road and the Carter very narrowly escaped. It continued all night of the first . . .

. . . until this morning. Saturday February 2nd when both the wind and snow abated.

2nd. Died Anne, wife of Philip Buckley of Burnley lane. She was his 3rd wife. Disorder a consumption. Age 24 years.

3rd. Died Hannah, daughter of Paul Ogden of Winnook age 16 weeks. This is the poor infant which was so miserably burnt . . .

. . . on the 14th of last month.

9th. Last night a most tremendous night of wind, frost and snow. The wind was higher and more terrific than that on the 1st and 2nd of this month. The Mail from London to Manchester was again stopped and the roads drifted full again and carts and other carriages stopped.

February 1799. 10th. This day Sunday the weather turned to a very fine thaw. Wind rose to a most astonishing degree and continued for the space of 24 hours. It blew an entire hurricane and was attended with a great deal of sleet and snow so that the air was . . .

. . . nearly darkened and it was not possible for persons to stir about business, and it terminated again into severe freezing, and Sergeant Taylor of the Norfolk Cavalry with 31 recruits passed down Burnley lane to join their Regiment at Edinburgh.

February 1799. 13th. The Frost was forced to give up its tyrannical and aggresive power to an agreeable and welcome thaw which commenced last night.

14th. Joseph Starkey Esquire of Royton, High Sherriff for the County of Lancaster this year.

Sir Rowland Wynne Bart of Nostel near Wakefield, Sherriff for Yorkshire this year.

5th. This day, James Collier of Northmoor was discharged from the New Bailey Prison, he having lain there three months for embezzling his work as Fustian piecer and during the above period he has been sworn in a private in the Duke of York's Invincibles.

February 1799. 11th. Three copies of 'The Sun' newspaper published at London was by order of the Irish Parliament burned by the hands of the Common Hangman in College Green in that city for publishing infamous lies.

In this month died William Tatton Esquire of Withinshaw Cheshire, a gentleman well known on the Jury.

20th. Last night some daring villians broke into the house of Edmund Radcliff, Nathan Row, Oldham and completely robbed it of everything portable and left not the least trace of discovery.

21st. Died Thomas Howard of Cowhill. He suddenly fell down at Rowbottoms Public House at Alder Root and died soon after. He died last night.

February 1799. 27th. Was observed as a general fast throughout England and Wales and indeed in consequence of the distressedness of the times the poor kept more fast days than the rich, although the rich strictly adhered to His Majestys Proclamation.

28th. Never in the memory of the oldest person living was weaving at a lower ebb . . .

. . . than at present, especially Fustians, for it is an absolute fact that goods within the last fortnight have lowered in Manchester Market astonishly, so that the Masters have lowered the wages at least 5 shillings a piece.

Excellent fine weather and has been for several days.

March 1799. 3rd. The consternation at Oldham is very great, in consequence of so many houses being broke and the perpetrators leaving no trace of discovery behind, for last night the dwelling house of John Marsland of Oldham was broke open and robbed of a large quantity of shoes and stockings with which they made of.

5th. Yesterday John Clegg, alias John Babby and . . .

. . . Worthington of Oldham were apprehended on supposition of breaking into the house of John Marsland of Oldham, and were taken before Sir Watts Horton, who committed them to the New Bailey to take their trial for the same.

10th. This morning died Thomas Kay of Old Clarks, a person remarkable for the inoffensiveness of his manners. He was far advanced in years.

March 1799. 10th. Last night and early this morning it fell a large quantity of snow and the wind was very high which caused the snow to be much drifted, and last night John Buckley, by his ingenuity and unparallelled dexterity and spirit made a clear escape from the hands of a posse of Constables.

March 1799. 14th. Yesterday a very large fall of snow, but the frost is very slight so that the sun soon dissolved the snow away.

19th. Yesterday a very large fall of snow, and Abraham Wild, Collier of Broadway lane died.

20th. Yesterday died Anne, relect of the late James Raynor of Top o'th'Moor.

March 1799. 12th. Delph, Saddleworth yesterday, the Coroners Inquest was taken of the bodies of two new born infants found under a haystack on the premises of Robert Bradbury, commonly called "Robin of Peers" of Peers near this place when it appeared, upon the testimony of Ann Hollinworth, who is daughter of the above Bradbury, that she was mother of the above infants and that he Bradbury the father had committed the . . .

. . . horrible sin of incest and was father of the above infants and that he had assisted her in her delivery and had taken these two innocents and murdered them. He was, of course, commited to York Castle to take his trial, and her taken care of in order to be evidence against him.

16th. Oldham this day, mutton raised in price from five pence, which price it has been for some time, to six pence a pound.

March 1799. 25th. Joseph Starkey, Esquire, High Sherriff set out from his house in Royton attended by the Oldham Fencable Cavalry and a band of music with a deal of his neighbours on his route for Lancaster. It should be observed that in the late severe weather the gentlemen of Oldham gave to the poor large quantities of coals and Pea soup which was a seasonable relief at that time.

March 1799. 30th. This morning the wind rose to an astonishing degree so as to resemble a hurricane. It came north east by east and froze so that it was extremely cold.

31st. The wind still continues to blow with the greatest velocity.

Although the last day of March, in consequence of the extreme cold weather, there is not the least appearance of Spring.

April 1799. 1st, 2nd, 3rd, 4th days of April, the wind still blows with the same velocity.

5th. Last night was one of the most terrific nights ever remembered by oldest person living. It begun early last night and continued its most triumphant career. The wind was astonishinaly high accompanied with a very large fall of snow. In consequence roads . . .

. . . were soon drifted up and carriages all sorts were stopped and it froze astonishingly so that it was scarcely ever equalled by the most tremendous frost in the depth of winter.

6th. Last night the wind as high as usual and rained at intervals. The rain was immediately froze to hedges and trees which made a very odd appearance and the roads were so slippery that it caused a deal of falls in the afternoon. The wind ceased for the first time since the 30th of last month. Wind all the time North East by East.

April 1799. On the 29th day of March ended the great Main of cocks betwixt Sir Watts Horton and Sir Rowland Wynne which was fought at Manchester and won by Sir Watts Horton.

14th. The weather still continues extremely cold and every day is attended with cold rain, hail or snow so that this has been one of the longest winters ever known by the oldest person living. Fodder of all sorts for cattle . . .

. . . is extremely scarce and dear, particularly hay which is now selling at fourteen pence per stone. As for Spring, there is not the least appearance of it, for vegetation has not made the least appearance and the poor warbling birds have not yet attempted by their sweet notes to usher in Spring. On the contrary they hop about as in the month of December or January and everything has a very dreary appearance.

April 1799. 13th. This day Manchester Quarter Sessions concluded when no Bill was found against John Clegg and Worthington for their charge - see the 22nd page - and this day, Saturday, the 'Angel Inn' Oldham was discovered to be on fire but, it happening early in the afternoon, a deal of people lent their assistance and the House very fortunately saved from destruction. Likewise a most singular genius was born this day in the person of B. Rowland.

15th. This morning the wind was most tremendously high, accompanied with a very severe frost. At night the wind dropped and it rained a little.

16th. Was an extreme fine day and the little warblers for the first time ushered in Spring.

17th. A cold chilly day as usual.

18th. Yesterday died James Rowland, grocer, Oldham. Age a little above 20 years. Disorder consumption.

April 1799. 20th. Died Mr.William Fletcher, Hat Manufacturer Oldham age about 30 years. Disorder consumption.

27th. Died John Clegg of Wood age 72 years. Disorder Jaundice.

Butchers Meat of all sorts is rising at an astonishing rate. Mutton is now selling at six pence halfpenny per pound, beef was sold at Manchester at . . .

. . . nine pence pound.

The extreme cold weather still continues and the hills still continue covered with snow.

30th. In consequence of the scarcity and dearness of hay and provender for cattle, Meal and Flour have taken a most rapid rise.

It still continues extremely cold. The wind as usual, East North East.

May 1799. 2nd. Oldham Spring Fair, a very cold, wet boisterous day. Very little business done and few company.

4th. The weather still continues extremely cold and very little appearance of grass so that it has caused a very great scarcity in food, for cattle hay is selling at from 14 pence to 16 pence . . .

. . . per stone. Straw 7 pence per stone, Bran dust, Shudes etc. extremely dear and scarce. Meal and flour is rising very fast.

17th. Ended Kersal Moor races which on the 16th, the Middle day were very numerously attended but owing to the coldness and wetness of this day, very few attended in consideration of it being the last days race.

16th. John Shepperd, cotton manufacturer of Heyside unfortunately killed . . .

. . . by his horse stumbling on a large stone at Middleton, as he was returning from the race.

18th. This morning was found hanging Robert Kay, of Lane End near Denton, he had been missing several days and is supposed to have committed this rash act a day or two before he was found.

21st. Large snow drift in consequence of the large . . .

. . . falls of snow last winter and this unparallelled cold spring there still remains on several hills in this neighbourhood large drifts of snow, particularly at Blackstone Edge. There is one which is very large and there is one which is very plain to be seen from Northmoor on one of the hills North.

31st. Every necessary of life is in consequence of this unparralled Spring in . . .

. . . a rising state. Meal sells at 2 shilling and 2 shilling and 2 pence a peck; flour about a penny peck higher, old butter 10 pence a pound, new butter 15 pence a pound in Manchester and a shilling a pound at Oldham. Beef and mutton seven pence halfpenny and eight pence a pound. Hay 15 pence a stone, straw seven pence a stone and all sorts . . .

. . . of provender dear and scarce. Fustian weaving every day worse and worse. (*38) All sorts of light goods extremely brisk and wages tolerable good. Hatting was never brisker in the memory of Man. Cotton wool still rises. Common weaving is now selling at 3 shillings and 2 pence a pound.

30th. The cold weather still continues to the detriment of vegetation.

June 1799. 4th. Was His Majestys birthday which was intended to have been ushered in with great pomp and festivity but it proved a very unfavourable morning by it raining which prevented a deal of public demonstration of Joy. Oak Branches, whose emblems of British loyalty could not this day . . .

. . . June 9th, be obtained. On the 29th May the Oaks, in consequence of the unparalled coldness of the Spring were just but beginning to bud so that Oldham Church Steeple was not this year adorned with the least particle of that branch. Some of the most loyal burning enthusiasts of the day made diligent search to have found a spring, but in vain, to the joy and triumph of the Jacobine party.

June 1799. 24th. This day the Oldham Association had their colours consecrated which were delivered by Miss Lees to the Major. The men fired some excellent volleys and the Rev. Mr. Winter preached a sermon on the occasion and Sarah Mills of Old Clarks died.

25th, was interred wife of Mr. John Fletcher, Hat Manufacturer Oldham and on the 6th of July 1799 died Mary, wife of William Haywood of Scolesfold, Maygate Lane.

July 1799. 6th. John Farrand of Oldham undertook for a wager to walk from Oldham to the Newcross Manchester, six miles and a half, in one hour and six minutes, which wager he won by three minutes.

13th. Died Mary, wife of William Halliwell of Northmoor. She had only been married twenty days, her disorder Convulsion Fits. Age 22 years.

14th. Delph, Saddleworth. This day Robert Bradbury and . . .

. . . Ann Hollinworth arrived from York Assize where they had been tried on a charge of murder but were acquitted (see page 26).

15th. A letter was received at Oldham from the East Indies giving an account of the death of John Needham and Benjamin Needham, Ammy Jonas, William Butterworth and wife, all of the 12th Regiment of Foot.

July 1799. 20th. Oldham this morning, John Clegg alias John Babby was apprehended for breaking into the dwelling house of Robert Mayall, grocer, and stealing a quantity of money. He was taken before the Magistrates who committed him for trial.

On the 27th, at the Sessions at Salford he was tried, found guilty and received sentence - seven years transportation. He is the same person mentioned in page 22 and 34.

July 1799. 31st. This month has in general been wet and cold and what little grass has been cut, it is feared it is much spoiled, for the Earth is so spongy and soft through the continual rain that if it comes a few hours sun it is naturally weakened by chilliness of the Earth. Potatos have thus far been both scarce and dear. On the 2nd of this month they were sold at Rochdale at four pence a pound the . . .

. . . finest sort, but they are sold at Oldham this day, one pound and a half for a penny. Gooseberries are exceeding scarce and are sold the finest sort for preserving five pence a Quart. Every necessary of life is extremely dear.

Cotton, such as is wove into velveteens is now selling at the amazing price of four shillings and two pence a pound, then great must be the miseries of poor fustian weavers.

Royton Hall

Page 52

August 1799. 2nd. Joseph Starkey, our worthy Sherriff, with his neighbours set out from Royton Hall to attend the Assizes at Lancaster which commence tomorrow. The Oldham Associated Cavalry attended early in the morning and one Richard Pimle walked from Oldham to Manchester in one hour and six minutes.

Page 53

August 1799. 9th. Judith, wife of Simeon Holding of Holdingfold interred at Royton this day. Last night or early this morning the Warehouse of Messrs. Cleggs, Hatters, Bent, Oldham was robbed of a large quantity of hats with which the villains made clear off.

14th. Died Thomas Rowland, Master of "The George Inn" Oldham. Disorder Consumption.

Page 54

16th. Yesterday an uncommon day for rain and wind which is very detrimental to the grass, both cut and uncut. There is the greatest quantity of grass ever known by the oldest person living. It is in most places a double crop but through the uncommon wet weather I am afraid a great deal of it will be spoiled . . .

Page 55

. . . for a wetter, colder, dirtier hay time was never remembered.

17th. Flood. On Saturday morning it began a-raining with the wind South. Sometimes it veered to South East. It rained to such a degree that the waters rose astonishingly, but at Craigh Clough it swept a Loomhouse away with such velocity that a part of the looms were found nearly at Middleton. At Chadderton its . . .

Page 56

. . . velocity was great and its appearance terrific. It swept away a house and threw the inhabitants into the greatest consternation. The innundation was general all over the country. In Saddleworth it swept three Bay of the large factory, situated at Bottom of Greenfield. It destroyed most of the Mill, wears, dams etc. All over the country swept away a great nurnber of bridges, swept a vast . . .

. . . quantity of hay and laid all lowlands under water and left them covered with mud, sand etc. Happily no person lost his life but some few cows horses and sheep lost their lives by the current washing them away. Upon the whole it was the greatest flood ever remembered in this country.

21st. Early this morning the celebrated pedestrian John Wood of Northmoor set . . .

. . . out from Oldham to walk to Manchester for a considerable wager. He set out from the Britannia Tavern and walked to the New Cross, Manchester. He was allowed one hour and four minutes but performed with ease in one hour one minute and thirty five seconds. Bets at starting 2 to 1 he won. An uncommon deal of wimberry this year, although they sold as high as four pence per Quart.

August 1799. 17th. The Bishop of Chester confirmed 6011 young people at Manchester this day.

28th. The wet weather still continues.

31st. Was Oldham Rushbearing Saturday which was a very wet cold day, and extreme few Company and owing to the wretchedness of the times there were only two Rush-carts viz one from Cowhill and one from Nimblenook.

September 1799. 1st. Was Oldham Rushbearing Sunday which was a very fine day and a tolerable deal of company.

2nd. Was Oldham Rushbearing Monday, a fine day and two Rushcarts are from Bent and one . . .

9th. The Archers commenced their annual shooting at Chadderton Hall. This day there was very few Archers and very little company.

21st. There has been about a fortnight of excellent fine weather which has made the Earth to smile, but within these few days it has again turned to bitter cold and rain which has caused meal and flour to rise astonishingly. Meal is now selling at Oldham as high as two shillings and two pence a peck, and flour at two shillings and eight pence a peck.

September 1799. 23rd. Extreme wet cold weather still continues and all the necessarys of life advancing. Weaving of all sorts is lowering, calicoes sixpence a cut, Fustian every day is still lower and lower. Great fall of cotton, this article of commerce the very best for weaving velveteens etc, is now selling at two . . .

. . . shillings and eight pence a pound and the inferior sorts betwixt two shillings and half a crown.

30th. The cold wet chilly weather still continues to the great detriment of all sorts of grain etc.

28th. Died wife of Joseph Poole, grocer Oldham. Disorder childbed.

October 1799. 7th. Died John Mills, Tailor, Chapel Street Oldham. Disorder Consumption.

5th. It is a shocking circumstance to relate that Meal is now selling from 2s & 3d to 2s & 5d per peck and flour from 2s & 8d to 2s & 10d per peck. Cotton, from 2s and 2s and 5d per pound.

13th. Select observations, the most dismal times . . .

. . . present to our view ever remembered. The season still continues so wet and cold that the fruits of the Earth are all blighted, crippled or starved for a great deal of flowers and grain have never ripened or come to perfection but have withered away, the same as untimely buds which sometimes bud at Christmas. Roses, Honeysuckle and a deal of flowering shrubs have perished before they . . .

. . . fully blowed or ripened. The air is cold as in December. The Earth is wet and soft as in a wet January. Everything has the most terrific and gloomy appearance such as never was known before. There is a deal of Corn-say oats which for lack of sun which will never ripen this season. Tradition says that the year 1735 was a similar year, but what must become of the poor? God have mercy on us.

October 1799. 14th. Oldham this day Meal sold at 2s and 7d a peck, flour 3s and 2d a peck and the Badgers in and about Chadderton sold this day Meal 2s and 8d a peck, 12 pound.

21st. Oldham this day Meal sold 2s and 6d a peck, flour 3s and 1d, apples 1s & 4d a peck, Damson plums 3 pence halfpenny a Quart, potatos 1s a stroke.

23rd. Last night died John Hilton of Holdenfold.

October 1799. 28th. This day at Oldham Meal sold from 2s & 7d to 2s & 8d a peck, 12 pound to the peck. Flour, the same as last week and this day a large mob of people from Saddleworth and the neighbourhood of Oldham assembled in Oldham who gave the Badgers notice to lower the price of flour and meal or else they would come on Thursday . . .

. . . next and retail out at a lower price. From thence they went peaceably home.

30th. Last night died Benjamin Ward, Butcher, Oldham. Disorder consumption.

31st. This day the mob assembled according to their promise and took all the meal and flour they could light on the road and sold it out. Flour 2s a peck and meal at 1s 8d per peck and reserved this morning for the owners.

November 1799. 1st. The mob assembled again on the new road leading to Ripponden. They came chiefly from Saddleworth and they took possession of eight loads of flour which was coming to Oldham, which they retailed out on the road at 2s a peck.

3rd. Died John, son of Daniel Bardsley of Maygate Lane age 23 years. Disorder, a fever.

November 1799. 4th. William Brierly of Chadderton fold in a fit of insanity drowned himself in a pond called Clogger pond. He was not found until the day following. Age 64 years.

4th. This day at Oldham Meal sold from 3s & 1d to 3s & 3d a peck.

11th. This day at Oldham Meal sold from 2s & 8d to 3s a peck. Flour 3s & 6d to 3s & 8d a peck.

November 1799. 13th. Last night Ellen Hide, alias 'Nell of Flutes' of Oldham, fell down the cellar steps at the 'Black Horse', Failsworth and was killed on the spot.

16th. Last night died Morton of Streetbridge. He had the misfortune to break his thigh a few days since and in consequence of it and this morning was found dead in a field near Nod, Chadderton, wife of . . .

. . . John Fenton of Chadderton. It is supposed she died in consequence of a fit.

17th. Died James Kay, Innkeeper New Road, Oldham.

18th. Oldham this day meal sold 3s & 4d a peck and flour 3s & 5d a peck, potatos 8s a load.

23rd. This Saturday at Manchester Meal sold 68s a load.

25th. Oldham this day Meal sold from 3s & 4d to 3s & 6d a peck, flour from 3s & 5d to 3s & 8d a peck.

November 1799. 30th. Manchester this day Meal sold from 62s to 63s a load and at Oldham Meal from 3s and 2d to 3s and 5d a peck, flour 3s & 8d a peck and cotton wool is now selling very good 1s & 10d. Cotton fit to be used in velveteens, Nineshafts etc. from 1s & 6d to 1s & 8d. Notwithstanding the price of Fustian pieces are monstrous low so that the poor weaver has from 3s to 5s less wages for a Velveteen than when cotton was 4s a pound and other sorts of fustians in . . .

. . . proportion. All sorts of light goods are extremely bad and very ill to be obtained by weaver. Calicoes are wove at 3s and some at 3s 6d per cut and to fill up the measure of our distresses I refer you to the price of provisions. Such is the distressedness of the times that it involves nearly all ranks of people. Most of the middling rank of people are Banking and the lower class are half starved. For want of provisions the poor little innocent children crying for bread.

December 1799. 7th. Manchester this day Meal sold from 58s to 60s a load, Flour 70s a load, potatos 7s a load and at Oldham Meal from 3s and 1d to 3s and 3d a peck, flour 3s & 8d.

9th. This morning died Mary wife of Daniel Bardsley of Maygate lane of a fever which most of that large family are and have been attacked with. Her age 46 years.

It is worthy of observation that since the beginning of November it has been as fine weather as ever was seen.

December 1799. 12th. Uncommon fine for both cutting corn and getting the wheat into the ground. It may seem extraordinary that corn is to be cut at this time but it is a fact that there is a deal of corn to cut in the Northern Counties. There were several acres of oats cut in this Parish the latter end of last month, particularly in the township of Crompton.

December 1799. 14th. Manchester this day Meal sold from 61s to 63s a load. Flour about the same.

16th. At Oldham provisions nearly same as last week.

14th. The uncommon fine weather still continues and it is remarkable that the Northmoor is as dry as in a fine month of March. The roads are so dry as to resemble a fine Spring.

21st. Manchester this day Meal sold from 66 to 68s a load. Flour about 70s a load.

December 1799. 23rd. Oldham this day Meal sold from 3s & 4d to 3s & 6d per peck and Flour 4s a peck, potatos 7s & 6d to 9s a load.

21st. Last night died James Lee, Badger, Maygate Lane, disorder Consumption.

22nd. Excellent fine weather still continues.

December 1799. 23rd. Last night it commenced a very fine frost and this morning, Beswick an apprentice of Coopers at the township of Crompton was found hanged in the Loomhouse. The Jury brought in their verdict: 'self murder' and he was in consequence buried in a lane near his Master's house.

December 1799. 28th. Manchester this day meal sold from 69s to 72s a load, flour from 72s to 75s a load.

The 23rd, 24th, 25th, 26th, 27th, 28th, 29th, 30th, it froze keenly with a very small quantity of snow, but the air was quite calm.

30th Oldham this day Meal sold from 3s & 7d to 3s & 9d, Flour 3s and 10d to 4s a peck.

December 1799. During this month subscriptions were opened in most of places in England for relieving the poor with bread etc.

In Oldham the poor received tickets which entitled them to a quantity of beef and potatos on paying one half value which was given on Wednesdays. The frost is very mild but still continues.

December 1799. Tuesday on the 31st it froze very keenly and ended the miserable year 1799, which year will forever be remembered as the most distressing miserable times ever experienced by the oldest person living, nay history does not produce an instance of such times.

The End

December 1799. Although it being the end of December, the Corn Harvest is but just finished. In Scotland and the Northern parts of England there is certainly corn out at this time belonging to Robert Scofield at Thornham in the Parish of Middleton. In the north they have practiced this. They have taken the corn when cut in the sheaf and set them Crop up and But end down upon a cool kiln which has . . .

. . . been found of great utility in drying & ripening the corn, but notwithstanding the corn is in general spoiled and is extremely light to the great distress of the poor.

FINIS

Oldham Church from Goldburn with a packhorse in the foreground

Notes On The Text

Alan Peat

1. The blockade of Carthagena under Admiral Edmund Blake was an early defeat for the English during the Seven Years War which began in 1756 and ended with the Treaty of Paris in 1763 in which the Franco-Austrian alliance was defeated by Britain and Prussia.

2. Rowbottom's Diary was originally edited by Samuel Andrew in the late 19th century. His transcript and notes were published in 'The Standard'. For this section of text I quote directly from Andrew's original notes:

"It was usual to saturate cotton with water when it had to be spun by hand in order to make it 'lick'. The cotton was weighed out by the piece master to the spinner, who first slubbed it between the finger and the thumb into a thick sliver, and then spun it in the same way into weft. The cotton was usually spread on a flake after being saturated and then placed before the fire to dry. Accidents of the kind here described were of frequent occurrence under the old system of domestic cotton spinning. A fire of this nature was no light matter though when we consider that the price of cotton was 2s to 3s per pound and the spinner, or spinster, would have to make the loss good".

3. Stang-riding was a Lancashire tradition, employed when a man or woman was caught committing adultery. Two long poles and a flat board were used to produce a kind of litter to which the offender was tied with ropes in a seated position. Four men then carried the adulterer through the local streets accompanied by a crowd beating pots, pans etc. to attract attention to the spectacle. As a further humiliation the leader of this procession would halt in front of all houses which were passed and loudly proclaim the names of the offending parties, as well as the time and location of the offence. If it proved to be impossible to catch the adulterers then a substitute would be found to stand-in for the real adulterer. It appears that in the instance mentioned in the text, Peter Blaze was acting as a substitute for Amos Ogden, seemingly to repay Ogden for his substitution for Blaze some 12 years earlier.

4. Bastardy was viewed as more of a sin against the Poor Law than against morality. Warrants were served when it appeared that the bastard child might become chargeable to the Parish. For a Bond to be served the pregnant woman had on oath to name the man who had "gotten her with child". The father would then be traced and placed in "the common gaol or some house of correction . . . unless he shall give security or indemnity". The entry for July 22nd 1789 gives us further information regarding the fate of the named father:

"James Woolstencroft, for bastardy was put in the new dungeon at Oldham and being the first inhabitant of this dreary mansion, received the charity of a gazing multitude". This passage seems to imply that the man committed for bastardy was put on view, a form of humiliation similar to stang-riding.

5. George III was King of Great Britain from 1760 to 1820. This passage refers to the King's recovery from his second major bout of manic depression. The first instance in 1765, he was ill again in 1788 (his recovery being marked in Oldham on March 19th). Two more serious attacks followed in 1801 and 1804 before he became permanently afflicted in 1811.

6. It is hard for us to imagine the landscape of Oldham and its environs prior to the Industrial Revolution. There are many short passages in Rowbottom's diary which help us to visualise a less industrialised environment. Otter hunts were frequent in the 18th century and if there were otters in the streams there were certainly fish for them to feed on.

7. Mayers were gangs of young men who went out on 'Mischief nect' (April 30th) playing tricks on their neighbours. A typical prank would be to take all of the loose items from a farmhouse and place them a distance away on the top of a hill. If it was easy to climb onto the roof then the items would instead be placed there. The 'Mayers' in this passage seem to have gone one step further in entering a house, hence the incident with the loaded gun.

8. The Duke's Cut is probably a reference to the Bridgewater Canal, built in 1761 by James Brindley. Work was still continuing on several branches of this canal in 1789.

9. The Battle of Dettingen (1748) was fought during The War of Austrian Succession of 1740-1748 and is remembered chiefly as the last battle in which a King of England led his troops in person. The King in question was George II.

10. A walk is a fulling mill, therefore a walk-miller is a person who is engaged in the process of fulling.

11. Supporters of the French Revolution are referred to throughout the diary as Jacobins. The riots mentioned in this passage took place on the anniversary of the storming of the Bastille on July 14th 1789.

12. After 1750 the speed of enclosure in Britain increased, much being done by Act of Parliament. Between 1770 and 1780 there were 660 acts, although this increased to approximately 1500 acts during the Napoleonic Wars, mainly due to rising prices for corn. Enclosure occurred in two major ways, firstly the consolidation of the individual strips which made up the open field system, and secondly the enclosure from commonground, woodland or waste ground. The latter caused the riot at Sheffield.

13. Bull baiting was a common spectacle in the late 18th century. The bull was tied to a post in an open area and, with the tips of its horns covered, was attacked by bulldogs. The bull would be driven into a frenzy whilst the dogs could easily be savaged or tossed. The sport was banned (along with bear-baiting) by an Act of Parliament in 1835.

14. Many societies similar to the Strangers' Friends Society were founded during the late 18th and early 19th Century, expressly to assist the poor. Their sufferings are chronicled by Rowbottom throughout this diary.

15. Strollers was a term used to describe men wandering from county to county in search of work. One of the duties of the constables was to take strollers into custody. For further duties see Note 18.

16. Although Rowbottom clearly sympathised with the poor he also often spoke highly of the local gentry. Sir Watts Horton was made High Sheriff of Lancashire in 1775 when still only 22 years of age, following in the footsteps of his father, Sir William Horton, who was High Sheriff of Lancashire in 1764 (the same year that he was knighted). The family lived at Chadderton Hall and feature on numerous occasions in the text.

17. An interesting point about this diary is that Rowbottom's character and opinions often come through in the text. The sentence which follows clearly demonstrates Rowbottom's thoughts concerning the character of fustian manufacture:

> "He was a fustian manufacturer, but character contrary to most,
> for he was sincerely a good man".

Most fustian manufacturers used pauper labour and this was possibly the root cause of Rowbottom's argument.

18. The constables and churchwardens would often walk through the streets during Divine Service in order to catch Sabbath breakers. Many were brought back to church. If, however, the Sabbath breaker was unfit to return to church (usually this meant 'drunk') then he or she would be placed in the stocks.

19. This short passage indicates the impact of Thomas Paine's "Rights of Man", written in three parts in 1791 and 1792 in reaction to Edmund Burke's "Reflections on the Revolution in France". Paine escaped England just before he could be arrested for treason and fled to France where he was elected to the new French Convention. See also Note 21.

20. Mr. Faulkner was printer of the Manchester Herald, a newspaper which opposed war with

France. The riot began with the mob merely chanting "God save the King", "Church and King", but soon led to the attacks on property mentioned in the text. Rowbottom's diary clearly paints a picture of the likely outcome which faced those who opposed war with France.

21. The burning of Thomas Paine's effigy is a remarkable insight into the formal way in which Oldham opposed the publication of 'Rights of Man'. The use of the 'dungeon' in the spectacle clearly suggests that the town officials were supporting this public condemnation of Paine and what he stood for.

22. News had just reached Oldham in February 1793 that France had declared war on England. It is for this reason that the number of men enlisting is so high.

23. In Samuel Andrew's late 19th century transcript of the text the following note was added concerning spotted fever;

"According to an old medical treatise, by Salmon, dated 1695, spotted fever was a continual malignant burning fever, the sick person being afflicted with great heat, thirst, and pains in the head and other parts of the body, after some days small spots coming out, sometimes all over the body, of a reddish purplish, livid, leaden or black colour, these spots being most visible where the larger veins and arteries do pass".

24. It is interesting that Rowbottom, as an eye-witness, clearly states that the reason for enlistment is the poverty of the hand-loom weavers.

25. The 33rd of Foot were referred to locally as the Haver Cake Lads. Oat cakes were colloquially known as haver cakes and the 33rd of Foot had as its emblem a haver cake speared on the end of the recruiting sergeant's sword. This regiment was raised in East Lancashire and the border of West Yorkshire.

26. Football was a popular game in Oldham sometimes being played over distances of up to five miles, the goals being placed at Lees and at Middleton.

27. This account once more demonstrates the dangers of being perceived as a Jacobin or French sympathiser. The 19th century historian Prentice adds a further detail in one of his sketches of Manchester, "There are numbers of persons now alive who recollect seeing in Manchester tavern's boards stuck up with the inscription - 'No jacobins admitted here' ".

28. The 29th of May was known as Royal Oaks Day. Oak boughs were attached to house doors to symbolise the patriotism of the inhabitants. These would have been seen as particularly important in the early years of the Napoleonic Wars.

29. The victory referred to in the text is the one that we know now as "The Glorious First of June". That victory was celebrated in Oldham so much later gives some indication of the time which information took to travel.

30. The Lancashire Fencebles were established by subscription in October 1794. Some indication of local patriotism (and also according to Rowbottom, poverty) can be gleaned from this entry as it suggests that more than 1000 men had joined the corps between October and December.

31. There are several entries in the diary which suggest that the Recruiting Officers took advantage of any event where people would gather. In this instance, the event is a bullbait, but we also find recruiting parties at fairs, festivals etc.

32. This entry demonstrates that the war with France did not elicit absolute support in Oldham. The Jacobins became more vocal as the war progressed, as can be seen in the main body of the text.

33. Bergen op Zoom was a Dutch fortress. The English and the Dutch were driven out in 1795 by the French. The paragraph also lists a large number of regiments returning to England after being beaten.

34. It is an indication of the hardship of the times that a substitute for flour was being sought in Oldham. Flour was doubly important in Lancashire, not only as a source of food but also for sizing the warps for weaving. The February 1796 edition of the Monthly Magazine for Lancashire states that:

"Many of the weaving manufacturers in this country have lately substituted potatos for fine flour in the process of deeting (smearing) their piece".

35. Hesse Cassel was a small independent German state. In 1807 it became part of Westphalia.

36. The Supplementary Militia Act was passed in 1796, followed by another in 1802. A quota of men between the ages of 18 and 45 was fixed for each county and these were raised by ballot (the lots mentioned in the text). The King had the power to call on The Militia, in case of rebellion or invasion, to join the regular army.

37. The Battle of Camperdown was fought off the Dutch coast on October 11th 1797 between the Dutch and English fleets. The English fleet's commander, Admiral Duncan was rewarded with the title of Lord Duncan of Camperdown.

38. Rowbottom is here chronicling the demise of the old domestic hand weaving industry and the rise of the new light goods made from weft spun by machinery. His descriptions of this industrialisation are of immense importance to the historian.

APPENDIX

Medical Terms From The Late 18th Century:

Ague:	used to define the recurring fever & chills of malarial infection
Aphonia:	laryngitis
Biliousness:	jaundice or other symptoms associated with liver disease
Camp Fever:	typhus
Canine Madness:	hydrophobia
Chlorosis:	iron deficiency anaemia
Corruption:	infection
Coryza:	a cold
Costiveness:	constipation
Cramp Colic:	appendicitis
Dropseyedema (swelling):	often caused by kidney or heart disease
Dyspepsia:	acid indigestion
Extravasated Blood:	rupture of blood vessel
Falling Sickness:	epilepsy
Flux of Humour:	circulation
French Pox:	venereal disease
Green Sickness:	anaemia
Hip Gout:	osteomyelitis
Jail Fever:	typhus
Kings Evil:	tubercular infection of the throat lymph glands
La Grippe:	influenza
Lues Venera:	venereal disease
Lumbago:	back pain
Lung Fever:	pneumonia
Lung Sickness	tuberculosis
Mania:	insanity
Mortification:	infection
Nostalgia:	homesickness
Putrid Fever:	diptheria
Quinsy:	tonsilitis
Remitting Fever:	malaria
Sanguineous Crust:	scab
Screws:	rheumatism
Scrofula:	see Kings Evil
Ships Fever:	typhus
Strangery:	rupture
Summer Complain:	baby diarrhoea caused by spoiled milk
Venesection:	bleeding